GROWING
INDOOR
PLANTS

GROWING
INDOOR
PLANTS

RONALD MENAGE

WARD LOCK LIMITED · LONDON

ACKNOWLEDGEMENTS

The publishers gratefully acknowledge the following agencies for granting permission to reproduce the colour photographs: Pat Brindley (pp 27, 30, 39, 46, 58 (top), 59, 63, 70, 75 and 87); the Harry Smith Horticultural Photographic Collection (pp 2, 14, 19, 22, 58, and 91); David Squire (p. 11). The cover photograph was taken by Bob Challinor, courtesy of Mr and Mrs D. Hayes.

© Ward Lock Limited 1987

First published in Great Britain in 1987
by Ward Lock Limited, 8 Clifford
Street, London W1X 1RB
An Egmont Company

House editor Denis Ingram

Text filmset in Bembo by
Paul Hicks Limited
Middleton, Manchester

Printed in Portugal

British Library Cataloguing in Publication Data
Menage, Ronald H.
    Growing indoor plants.—2nd ed.
    1. House plants
    I. Title
    635.9'65   SB419
    ISBN 0–7063–6513–5

Frontispiece: Thunbergia alata can be grown as a climber or trailer and is very easy from seed.

CONTENTS

PREFACE

There are many books on house plants, but the majority deal with a large number of plants that often fail to thrive unless given ideal conditions and considerable care. This book aims to draw attention to the easier plants and those able to survive some neglect. It also introduces the more simple ways to grow your own house plants cheaply from seed or from bulbs and cuttings, without necessarily having the facility of a garden, greenhouse, or frame.

Tips on the general care of house plants are given, and on the best ways to use them and to display them in the home. Common mistakes are drawn to attention, and in the text there will be found numerous modern and absolutely up-to-date techniques and products. Where possible modern plant varieties that are improvements on the old are recommended, since plant breeders are always striving for better general plant quality.

All plants and materials described are available. Most can be obtained from good garden shops and centres, but a list of useful addresses is given in the Appendix.

PUBLISHER'S NOTE

Readers are requested to note that in order to make the text intelligible in both hemispheres, plant flowering times, etc. are generally described in terms of seasons, not months. The following table provides an approximate 'translation' of seasons into months for the two hemispheres.

NORTHERN HEMISPHERE				SOUTHERN HEMISPHERE
Mid-winter	=	January	=	Mid-summer
Late winter	=	February	=	Late summer
Early spring	=	March	=	Early autumn
Mid-spring	=	April	=	Mid-autumn
Late spring	=	May	=	Late autumn
Early summer	=	June	=	Early winter
Mid-summer	=	July	=	Mid-winter
Late summer	=	August	=	Late winter
Early autumn	=	September	=	Early spring
Mid-autumn	=	October	=	Mid-spring
Late autumn	=	November	=	Late spring
Early winter	=	December	=	Early summer

Measurements are generally cited in metric followed by the imperial equivalent in parentheses. In a few instances, owing to pressure on space, the imperial equivalent has been omitted.

CHAPTER 1

USING PLANTS TO DECORATE THE HOME

When a house is decorated or furnished care is taken to see that styles and colours blend to give a pleasing harmonious appearance. The best effect is obtained if the plants are selected with the same consideration. However, it is important to see that any plants chosen will be happy in their environment. A room, or the house as a whole, usually provides a variety of different conditions. There will be dark and bright places, cool or draughty spots, warm sites, and various facilities of space and height. Make sure that your plants are suited to them. Also, don't forget to use the colours and shapes of plants, and their habit – such as climbers, trailers, and other forms – to fit in with your décor or furnishing. Best sites for plants are suggested as they are described, but the following points should be remembered.

ROOMS, CORRIDORS, LANDINGS AND HALLWAYS

When choosing plants for rooms the amount of light entering is the most important consideration. In some cases too, there may be wide temperature fluctuations. For example, a living room may be unheated during the weekdays, but become quite warm at weekends and evenings when the room is occupied. There are very few plants that will do well in perpetual gloom. If you have a very dark corner, try using artificial light as described in Chapter 8. Sometimes a gloomy spot can be made to catch and reflect light by fixing mirrors or mirror tiles to the wall. This may make a display of plants more attractive too. Homes with central heating often have rather dry air: plants will flourish in congenial warmth provided the air is reasonably moist. Ways to achieve this are described in Chapter 2, but to get the air moist generally, humidifiers can be bought to attach to radiators. There are also electrically controlled automatic types.

Coal gas is poisonous to plants, so the introduction of natural gas, which has no toxic effect on them, means that homes with open gas fires can enjoy both flowers and foliage in the home. However, plants should not be put where they receive direct heat radiation either from gas or electric fires – otherwise they will suffer leaf scorch.

Bedrooms are often good places for plants since the temperature remains fairly constant. Provided the room is reasonably ventilated there is no need to be afraid of plants using up the oxygen of the air. The business of removing flowers and plants from rooms at night is rather nonsensical!

Corridors and passages may be draughty and they often suffer from lack of light. If simple measures like keeping doors closed with spring or pneumatic closing devices will reduce draughts the plants will be much happier – even if they are of some of the hardy types recommended later in the book. Landings often have windows to give good illumination to stairways and may provide excellent conditions for relatively large leafy plants. Hallways may have space and, if there is a stair-well, offer considerable height. Any entrance to a home will welcome visitors if a rather grand grouped display of plants can be arranged. For stair-wells climbing plants can often be used with pleasing effect. In a hallway, take advantage of the space to allow impressive plants like palms or Ficus (rubber plants) to show their splendour.

In most parts of the home walls can be decorated with plants in hanging containers if there is sufficient light. Trailing plants can also be allowed to cascade from pots on shelves or on room dividers of the type consisting of shelves one above the other. In some cases plants can be grown in pots or containers suspended from arched ceilings or the top of windows.

WINDOWS AND WINDOW SILLS

Because of the good light conditions, positions in or near windows will be found ideal for a wide range of house plants. The choice of type depends on how much light enters, and this may be governed by curtains or window design and particularly by which way the window faces. Suitable plants can be found for either very sunny windows – which can sometimes become very warm – or those facing north and perhaps hardly ever getting much sunshine. Sunny windows can of course be shaded if necessary, or if desirable, with interior blinds or the exterior awning type (Fig. 1). Net curtains will also afford some protection from the sun without cutting out too much light or the view from the window.

In some cases it is tempting to crowd a window with plants, but this should not be done so as to obscure light entry into a room or a pleasant view from the window. However, if there is more than one window to

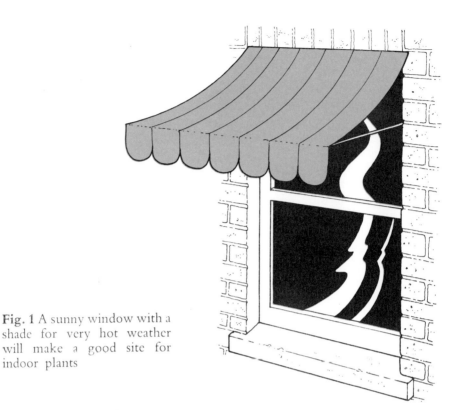

Fig. 1 A sunny window with a shade for very hot weather will make a good site for indoor plants

a room it may be possible to devote at least one of them to plant growing.

Window sills are best covered with some water resistant material as a precaution. Tiles, or laminated plastic are usually suitable, but additional trays or saucers will still be necessary to catch any excess water that escapes from pots when watering, unless proper plant containers are used.

Windows can become very chilly at night – even frosty – and double glazing is an obvious advantage. However, in some cases where the inner panes are hinged lots of pots in front can be a nuisance when it comes to opening or cleaning the window. In windows subject to excessive chill in winter, remember to move plants back from the glass at night or pull curtains *during the hours of darkness only* – otherwise plants will become pale and weak. To get more plants into a window area, plate glass shelving can be fitted if the window design allows.

GARDEN ROOMS AND CONSERVATORIES

In recent years home extensions of the erect-yourself pre-fabricated type have become very popular and are usually set against a door, or

Aechmea fasciata, a bromeliad with attractive foliage and showy long lasting bracts.

French doors, leading to the garden. These home extensions make an excellent environment for growing plants. However, if the room is to be lived in the plants must be kept in check and used with discretion. Often the room is mostly regarded as a sun lounge or an extension to the garden and plants can then be used more freely. Because such home extensions are usually sited to get as much sunlight as possible, the plants should be chosen to like warm bright sunny conditions and a dryish atmosphere in summer. Succulents and cacti are ideal where there is a lot of sunlight.

Many prefabricated garden rooms have corrugated plastic roofing with not much slope. This means that if the humidity is high condensation forms and drips from the corrugations. Humidity will be raised if there are many plants needing watering in winter and the temperature is fairly warm, and also if *non-flued* paraffin or gas heaters are used for heating. Paraffin and gas produce water vapour when they burn and this will condense, forming water droplets, unless there is reasonably good ventilation. For garden rooms a dry heat such as electric fan heating is preferable.

A conservatory makes a splendid home for many house plants and there are numerous hardy plants that can be grown in a conservatory that is without any artificial heat in winter – since they need only protection from wind, excessive rain, and exceptional cold, which might damage foliage or flowers but not kill the plants. Generally the difference between a conservatory and a garden room is that whilst in a garden room the plants take a second place and the comfort of the human inhabitants comes first, a conservatory is a home for plants where every attempt is made to keep them decorative the year round and people are more regarded as privileged visitors.

A conservatory need not be sited to get full sun, and a shady place, perhaps facing north, is often ideal. Most conservatory plants do not like hot sunny conditions, and may be short-lived or wilt badly if these occur.

EXPLOITING PLANT HABIT AND COLOUR

Full advantage should be taken of the fact that plants have a wide variety of habit – that is, they have many shapes and forms. Some grow to form a bush shape or it may be possible to train them to take forms like pyramids or standards, others may trail or hang, and there are numerous climbers and plants that can be grown up supports. The height of plants and their leaf size may have to be taken into account, and there is tremendous variety of leaf shape. Leaf texture – glossy,

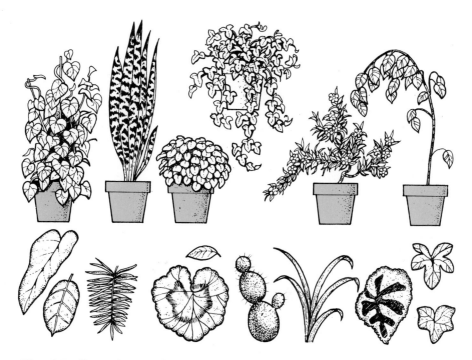

Fig. 2 Different kinds of plant habit and the enormous variety of leaf shapes offer wide opportunities for skill in arrangement

hairy, or velvety, may be useful too when choosing plants to blend or contrast with furnishings. Colour is very important and useful. Coleus for example will give very many hues and it is nearly always possible to select some wonderful colours, from plants derived from a packet of 'mixed' seed, to match any home colour scheme. Seed of many 'self' colours is also now available.

Most house plants are evergreen, but those with variegated foliage are also extremely desirable. There are lots with combinations of green shades and cream, and these will brighten and add interest to dreary corners as well as enhancing groups of plain foliage plants (Fig. 2).

Flowering house plants are obviously highly favoured. A number of easy ones are brought to attention in this book, but a wider selection can be achieved if you have a frame or small greenhouse where many flowering plants can be raised in ideal conditions merely to decorate the home when they are ready for display. Numerous flowering plants sold as 'house plants' by florist's shops are in fact short-lived in the home and include azaleas, cyclamen and pot chrysanthemums which are not particularly attractive when dormant. Again a frame or greenhouse is the place for them when out of flower. It is wise to choose flowering house plants that also have attractive *evergreen* foliage. You will then enjoy them the year round.

Caladiums are grown from tubers for glorious summer foliage. Store dry over winter.

CHAPTER 2

CONTAINERS AND THE DISPLAY OF PLANTS

Choosing the right kind of pot or container and how the plants are displayed has a dramatic effect on how effective they appear – and on their wellbeing. However beautiful a plant, an ugly or clashing container can cause a distraction. Consideration must also be given to the drainage of pots and their composition and various technical aspects if the plants are to be made happy (Fig. 3). The grouping of several plants and their support if necessary is also important both to appearance or artistic presentation, and to their health and vigour.

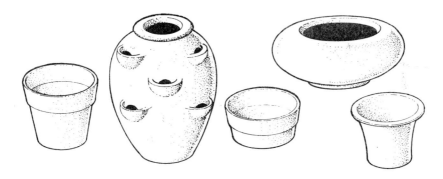

Fig. 3 Some of the different types of container available – check that those you choose are adequately drained

VARIOUS TYPES OF PLANT CONTAINER AND THEIR CHOICE

House plants are usually bought or raised in plastic pots nowadays. Always examine the bottom of the pot and check whether roots can be seen in the drainage hole or emerging from it. If this is the case the plant may need potting-on to a slightly larger pot as described in Chapter 3. A plant may appear too large for its pot, but do not be tempted to pot-on unless it is really necessary and always avoid giving a plant pots that are unnecessarily large. If when examined the drainage hole of a pot is seen to be covered from the inside with a 'crock' (see page 31) which would obscure roots from view, it may be informative to tap the plant out of its pot as described on page 28. If the root ball is then seen to be excessively matted with roots and the roots are winding around the pot sides with little potting compost surrounding them, it is time to pot-on. The plant is then described as 'pot-bound'. This sort of examination is specially necessary when a plant is first bought, since nursery and shop plants are often pot-bound. Whether the plant should be potted-on or not will help in choosing and deciding on its future pot type, size, and sort of container.

Plastic flowerports have many advantages over the old clay pots and a few disadvantages. They are very easy to keep clean and do not collect slime and algae or white mineral deposits on the outside. They are lightweight and easily stored, demanding little space, and they can be obtained in a variety of shapes and colours – which can be useful if no outer covering pot is to be given to the flowerpot. Disadvantages that can be noted are a tendency for old plastic pots to split if not handled carefully (especially if the pots have been exposed to direct sunlight for some time), the colours to fade on exposure to light, and their light weight causing a tendency for large tall plants to become unstable and topple over.

Because plastic pots are non-porous, the roots of plants dry out more slowly than if they were in clay porous pots. This is an advantage since watering needs to be less frequent, but if you have been used to clay pots *be careful not to overwater.*

PLUNGING PLANTS

Plunging plant flowerpots is an ideal way to give excellent conditions for plant growth in the home. As well as peat and vermiculite any other suitable moisture-retaining substance can be used. *Clean* sand or grit washed free from any lime it may possibly contain, the mineral material 'pearlite' sometimes used on greenhouse staging and for rooting cuttings, or any other clean material that holds water well and will not rot or decay, can be employed.

The plunge material is held in an ornamental container with no drainage holes so that there is no fear of excess water running out onto furnishings. Most garden shops have a wide selection of suitable containers and they may take the form of large bowls, made from plastic or pottery, timber tubs, plastic troughs sometimes on ornamental stands, and reproduction or genuine antique jardinières. Since plunging is usually done when it is desired to group plants, the

Fig. 4 Plunging pots create good growing conditions – the rims can be just covered with the plunging material

container must obviously be large enough to take the pots allowing several inches of the plunge material between them. It must also be deep enough so that the deepest pot can be immersed to cover the rim (Fig. 4). If plastic pots are to be plunged, it is best to have the plunge material well over the top in contact with the potting compost. Moisture will then travel into the pot compost from the moist plunge material and there will be less tendency for plants to dry out quickly. Pots should, however, be well crocked to prevent roots from passing through into the plunge material. If they do there will be much mess and inconvenience when it is necessary to change the plants, in addition to root damage.

As well as giving a pleasing natural appearance, and obscuring flowerpots, the plunge keeps plants nicely and evenly moist over a long period. The water that evaporates from the plunge also maintains a localized humid atmosphere which is extremely beneficial to most plants.

Next best to the plunge method is to stand the flowerpot containing the plant in a decorative outer one. This is not a modern idea – the Victorians used to use elaborate decorated glazed pots called 'art pots'. Originals can still be found expensively priced in antique shops. Most stores and garden shops have plastic equivalents of the old 'art pot' and containers made in a variety of materials, now often called 'planters'. Drainage holes are of course *not* wanted, but the inner pots should always be raised on any suitable supports – such as a few pebbles – so

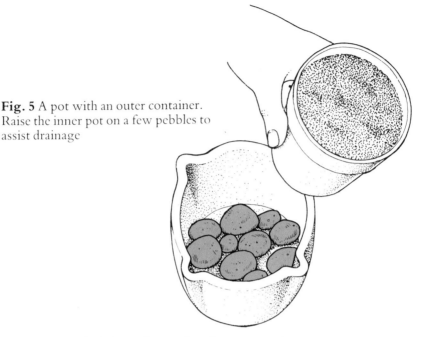

Fig. 5 A pot with an outer container.
Raise the inner pot on a few pebbles to
assist drainage

that water draining from the flowerpot does not cause constant
saturation of the plant's potting mix (Fig. 5). With very few exceptions,
plants must never be stood in water for any length of time.

If you collect many house plants and have them scattered about the
home, it is inevitable that some will have to be grown in ordinary
flowerpots stood on saucers where it is not possible to find room for a
'humidity tray'. To improve appearance the conventional type of
flowerpots can now be obtained in numerous colours, but garish
clashing colours should be avoided. The most common are terracotta
(the colour of clay pots), green and black. Both green and black tend to
fade after a time. Sometimes white pots can be found and are most
desirable, since white goes well with all plant colours and gives a clean
elegant effect. Food products are often packed in small tubs that make
excellent pots. The print can usually be easily removed by brisk
rubbing with a wet cloth and a domestic abrasive powder, leaving a
pleasing pure white surface. Holes for drainage can be made in the
bottom with a hot poker or similar object. Some butchers have large
kegs and pots of white plastic in which liver and offal are packed. These
can be cleaned and make splendid pots, being large enough to be used
as outer pots too if no drainage holes are made. By enquiring, you may
be able to get these spare pots quite cheaply. Such containers, and
similar types, can also be 'ornamented' with self adhesive vinyl as used
for lining shelves, and available from most DIY shops. Saucers on

Saintpaulia ionantha or African Violet is now available in many forms and colours.

Cineraria 'Spring Glory' is obtainable in many other rich colours apart from the one shown.

which to stand pots can often be obtained very cheaply from the 'bargain box' of junk shops and are often preferable to special plastic saucers sold for the purpose by garden shops.

A word of advice may be helpful regarding metal 'art pots' or outer pots of the copper or brass type. These look very beautiful and make very attractive containers for plants. New ones can be bought, but antique types are common, and old 'helmet' coal buckets are used as well as a variety of other copper or brass domestic containers often of Victorian times. Do not stand ordinary flowerpots in them so that water draining from the pot can contact the metal directly. It will contain fertilizer salts and other minerals from the potting mix that can cause severe corrosion after a time. Use your decorative metal container as a *third* extreme outer pot, placing the pot in which the plant is growing in another undrained pot so that water is kept out of contact with the material.

SELF-WATERING POTS AND TROUGHS

For minimizing watering attention, but also helping to keep plants evenly watered, a number of designs of automatic watering containers can be bought. Both relatively small pot-sized containers and troughs holding a number of plants can be obtained. Usually these containers have a concealed water reservoir. Water from these is conveyed to the compost in the plant pots by a wick system (Fig. 6). Sometimes the plants can be plunged in the larger automatic watering containers, the plunge material then being kept moist automatically. These devices are especially useful to those who tend to overwater.

Fig. 6 A self-watering pot – note the wick

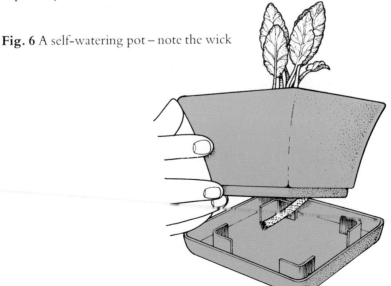

SUPPORTING, TRAINING, POSITIONING AND GROUPING

Just as important as the container is the way plants are supported if necessary, what shape they are allowed to take and grow into, and how they are grouped or positioned.

The majority of house plants are reasonably neat growing, fairly short in height, and compact. However, when a plant with height is required it is always best to give some form of support (Fig. 7). A sudden draught from an opened window or door, or moving about during cleaning, can easily cause a brittle stem to snap. The old-fashioned bamboo cane is still one of the best supports in many cases. It looks pleasant, blending well with most plants, and has considerable strength. Split cane, which is thinner and more suited to small plants, is also strong and is often coloured green. Some plants that have foliage tending to flop and become untidy may need several canes set around the pot edge with an inconspicuous thread wound around. It will be appreciated that all tying must be as neat as possible. Green plastic-coated wire is generally most useful for a wide range of plants, and green thread for those where the tie must be as inconspicuous as possible. A number of patent plant ties are sold by garden shops and may be found useful at times. If heavy stems of plants need to be supported, because they are carrying flowers or much foliage, it is sometimes better to use a narrow *tape* which will not cut

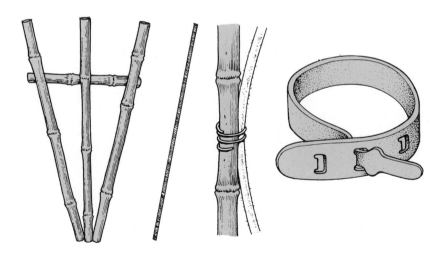

Fig. 7 Different kinds of plant support

Campanula isophylla is a charming plant for hanging containers. There's also a blue form.

into the stem.

For low growing, but straggly plants, short twiggy sticks cut from outdoor shrubs and small trees can be found useful – but they may introduce garden pests and diseases and should be cleaned thoroughly before use.

For climbing house plants special plastic mesh can be bought designed for insertion into pots, but it is usually only suited to small climbers like the compact type ivies, and *Thunbergia alata* (page 65). For taller plants bamboos are again suitable and can be arranged with three or four placed fan-wise for the plant to be tied to. Some climbers will be self-supporting by twining or by sending out tendrils – but it is wise not to rely entirely on such natural support. Others will have to be supported artificially from the earliest stages. Plants that form aerial roots, like philodendron and monstera, become self-supporting if grown up a mossy pole for the roots to penetrate. This is made by binding a stout bamboo cane with sphagnum moss secured with florists' wire. The mossy support should be kept moist by spraying with water from time to time.

Climbers are sometimes allowed to attach themselves to permanent parts of the house structure. This is rarely a good idea because the plants may grow to a considerable size and there will be much damage to the plant if it ever needs moving. Sometimes exudations from plants – sap, nectar, pollen, and suchlike – can spoil paintwork or wall decoration.

All tall plants are liable to become top-heavy, especially when lightweight pots of plastic, and the modern peat-type potting composts are used, and more so when the compost is on the dry side. Using heavy outer pots will help, or some stones can be put in to increase weight. Alternatively, the John Innes loam-based compost (page 90) can be used when potting, perhaps with a clay pot.

For plants that are of a pendant or trailing nature, special non-drip baskets can be obtained for hanging (Fig. 8). You can also make your own hanging containers by making holes with a hot wire around a suitable outer plastic pot and fixing wire supports. Special non-drip wall pots can be bought too, and also wrought iron plant stands to give trailing plants height. Sometimes standing a plant on an inverted pot will give enough room for the plant to trail and conceal its support.

Very low-growing or compact plants may look ridiculous in the conventional tall pot. For these what are known as half-pots, or alpine pots, are in better proportion, and can be stood in shallow outer containers.

A group of plants looks much more exciting if several plant heights,

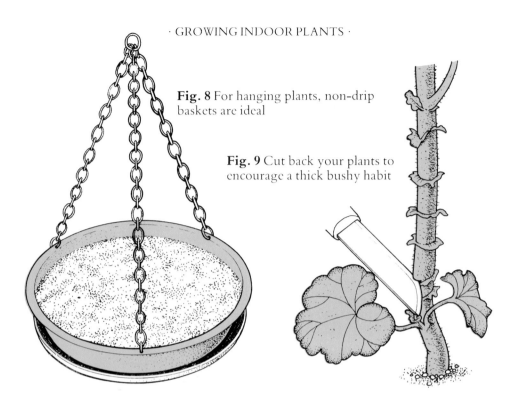

Fig. 8 For hanging plants, non-drip baskets are ideal

Fig. 9 Cut back your plants to encourage a thick bushy habit

and contrasting foliage are used. By grouping in a plunge (page 16) it is easy to adjust plant height. Moreover, it is simple to change plants if they deteriorate or grow too large – or you just feel like making a different display. Sometimes plants that have lost lower foliage or become 'leggy' – this happens from time to time – are useful in a group; the lower parts can be obscured by other plants, and the top foliage will rise above, perhaps making the plant look far more impressive than if the whole were visible. Plants trained as standards can be used too, but these are nearly always best displayed on their own.

The training of standard plants like fuchsias, geraniums or marguerites, is really a greenhouse gardener's technique, but simpler training can be carried out on most plants. Many house plants become straggly and untidy – *never be afraid to cut these back or to cut off growing tips.* This will induce new shoots to grow from lower down and you will soon have nice bushy and compact plants. A typical example so frequently seen is the 'geranium' (zonal pelargonium) on the window sill. This is often allowed to grow to the most absurd height, bearing leaves and flowers on many barren straggly stems. If the plants were literally murdered, by severe cutting back an inch or so from the base, new compact neat growth would soon result (Fig. 9) Trailers like tradescantias, *Zebrina pendula*, and *Setcreasea purpurea*, also benefit from

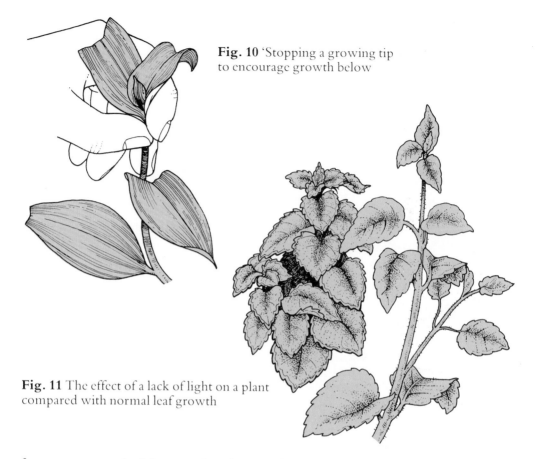

Fig. 10 'Stopping a growing tip to encourage growth below

Fig. 11 The effect of a lack of light on a plant compared with normal leaf growth

frequent removal of the growing tips – or 'stopping' as this operation is called professionally (Fig. 10).

An unsatisfactory site will often affect a plant's appearance although not actually causing drastic ill health. The colour or leaf variegation may be affected, as may flowering and height. Best positions are given under the descriptions of plants in Chapters 4, 5 and 6, and special attention drawn to those plants greatly affected by light. Generally, however, poor light or heat will encourage lanky growth and paler leaf colouring (Fig. 11). It may in some house plants reduce or even inhibit flowering. A pale leaf colour can also occur in plants that like shade when they receive too much light. In this case a kind of bleaching takes place. A successful house plant grower will always experiment regarding position, more especially when trying plants for the first time. The way to grow good plants is by using your *eyes* and being observant of their reaction to various conditions.

CHAPTER 3

GENERAL CARE OF HOUSE PLANTS

Not all house plants will live to become antiques like the aspidistra, but many will give pleasure for years if given reasonable care. Often, like us, plants deteriorate with age or outgrow their pots. This cannot be prevented, and invariably the answer is to use the parent plant to propagate new young stock. Chapter 7 describes day to day general care starting from the beginning when a plant is acquired. It should help you to keep your plants looking attractive and greatly aid the enjoyment you get from them.

BUYING AND ACQUIRING HOUSE PLANTS

An interest in house plants is often started through cuttings or gifts of plants being passed on by friends. Always be a little wary of such presents, since they may well be derived from plants that tend to become rampant and perhaps a little too frequently seen. A special offering to refuse politely is a cutting of impatiens, busy lizzie (see page 61). You can raise free-flowering plants of this and many others yourself. However if a friend has some particularly delightful house plant you may well able to beg a cutting and root it as described in Chapter 7, or ask for a piece of root to be saved for you if the plant has to be divided at any time.

The best way to obtain plants is to purchase from a reputable nursery or florist. Most of the house plants described in this book can be bought at any time; the ideal time to obtain plants is spring. It should be realized that plants bought from ordinary shops may have been left about in very adverse conditions, or neglected for some time. The ill effects of such treatment may only appear after you have taken the plant home. Falling leaves or flowers and wilting or yellowing of foliage could be a delayed result of chill or lack of water. Winter purchases may also mean transport through the cold which is also best avoided. Obviously any plant showing signs of ill health or the presence of pests must be strictly shunned. Check for leaf yellowing and particularly mottling which could mean virus disease or red spider attack (see pages 38 and 40) and always look under the foliage where pests tend to first

Azaleas with chlorophytum in the background.

Clivia miniata is an impressive plant with huge umbels of bright orange trumpet flowers.

congregate. When you get the plant home check whether it may need a larger pot as described on page 15.

POTTING AND POTTING COMPOSTS

A flowerpot should always be kept as small as possible. Overlarge pots look ridiculous, they make it difficult to find outer decorative containers – and they hold an excess of potting compost, wasting money and resulting in the compost becoming stale and washed free from nutrients by the time the plant roots penetrate. Provided a proper potting compost is employed and the plants are fed, large pots are unnecessary (Fig. 12). A smallish pot is often a special advantage with

Fig. 12 Never put plants in containers that are too big for them

flowering annuals grown as house plants. In this case, being slightly pot-bound, the freedom of flowering is often increased by the plant attempting to produce seed for survival of the species. However, when it is necessary to pot-on to a larger pot, a pot size giving about an inch or so extra compost around the root ball should be chosen.

To remove a plant from its pot turn it upside down in one hand, allowing the plant stem to pass through the fingers. A sharp tap on the pot rim using a suitable object held in the other hand will usually cause the root ball to slip out of the pot easily (Fig. 13). Large pots will have to be held in both hands and the pot rim tapped on the edge of a bench or table, again holding the plant upside down so that the pot will not fall to the floor.

GARDEN SOIL MUST NEVER BE USED FOR POTTING – this is of the utmost

Fig. 13 Removing a plant from its pot

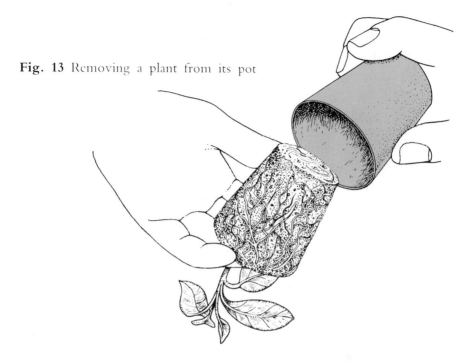

importance. If you do there will be certain trouble from pests, diseases, and weeds. Nowadays there are numerous specially formulated potting mixes which are sterile and contain carefully balanced plant foods to give first class growth over a long period. Proprietary potting composts can be bought from most garden shops and are usually based on peat. The original potting compost was invented by W. J. C. Lawrence and J. Newel of the John Innes Horticultural Institute. It is still an ideal compost and can be bought ready made, but it must be genuine and obtained from a reliable supplier. It uses sterilized loam, peat, and washed grit, mixed with nutrients and chalk (see Appendix) and is consequently much heavier than the peat composts, giving greater stability to tall plants. There are several grades – No. 1, No. 2, and No. 3 being most employed. The numbers relate to the fertilizer content and for house plants No. 2 is generally the best. Very slow-growing plants could have No. 1 and vigorous plants No. 3, but for house plants the No. 3 is rarely needed.

Another useful potting compost has been devised by the University of California. This is based on peat and grit and its formula is given in the Appendix in case some readers may have the facilities to make it themselves. You can also make a relatively simple potting compost by mixing three parts by volume of moss peat with one part of washed

Coleus is one of the most colourful foliage plants you can raise easily from seed.

grit, and adding to every 13 cm (5 in) potful one level teaspoon of Phostrogen soluble fertilizer, available from most garden shops, and the same amount of powdered chalk. The chalk can be omitted for some plants (see below).

The potting composts are designed and formulated to suit a very wide range of different plants, and the standard composts contain chalk. Some plants, however, are lime haters and its presence will cause poor growth and yellowing foliage. For these the chalk should be omitted from a compost if this is possible. Alternatively specially *acid* composts can be asked for at garden shops, since some firms now supply them. Plants needing acid compost are mentioned in Chapters 5 and 6, as well as those preferring unusual or special composts.

Use only clean flowerpots for potting. Plastic pots are easy to wash, but clay pots may need soaking by complete immersion in water at least overnight before any mineral deposits can be scrubbed off. Do not use dry clay pots for potting. The dry clay can absorb much moisture from the potting compost.

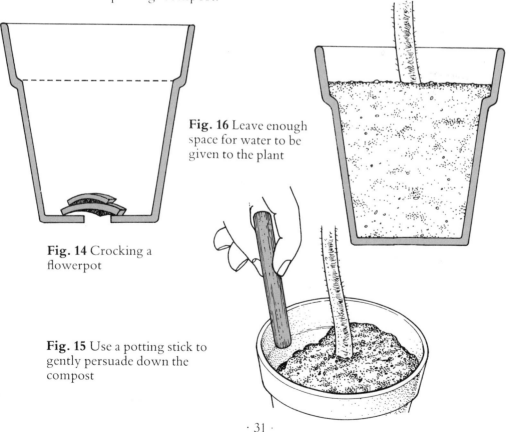

Fig. 16 Leave enough space for water to be given to the plant

Fig. 14 Crocking a flowerpot

Fig. 15 Use a potting stick to gently persuade down the compost

The first step when potting is to make sure there is perfect drainage. The drainage hole of the pot must be covered to prevent compost falling out but to allow free flow of any excess water. It can be covered with a few pieces of broken pot, or specially perforated zinc disks can be purchased (Fig. 14). If drainage is particularly important a few clean pebbles can be placed on top. With the exception of certain cases involving planting bulbs in ornamental containers (see page 47), undrained pots without drainage holes must not be used, as without drainage there is risk of waterlogging and rotting of the plant roots.

After crocking, a little potting compost – *which must always be moist, but not wet* – is put at the bottom of the pot. The depth must be such that the plant's stem base will come to a point about half an inch below the pot rim. The space around the plant's root ball is then filled with more potting compost. This can be gently persuaded down with a piece of stick (called a potting stick) and tapping the pot on a bench – but the compost must not be rammed down or firmly compressed (Fig. 15). Common sense should be applied so that the compost is not so loose that the plant can rock about, or too firm so that peneration of water and air to the roots and drainage is inhibited.

The space of about 1 cm (½ in) between the compost surface and the pot rim is to allow water to be applied without spilling over the pot sides and helps in assessing how much water is given (Fig. 16).

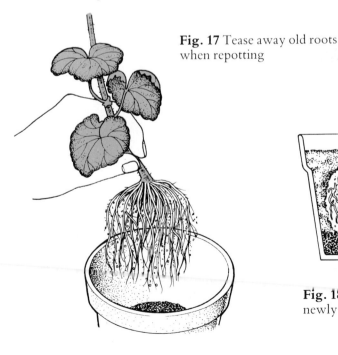

Fig. 17 Tease away old roots when repotting

Fig. 18 Section through a newly potted-on plant

Obviously a plant cannot be potted on indefinitely. There consequently comes a time when many plants benefit from *repotting*. In this case the plant is removed from its pot and the root ball considerably reduced in size by carefully teasing away the compost and old roots (Fig. 17). It is then potted with fresh compost *in the same size pot*. This gives encouragement for new roots to grow, but the process must be done at a time of year when the plant is about to start into new growth – usually early spring (Fig. 18).

WATERING

All pot plant specialists agree that overwatering is the chief cause of failure. Saturated compost cannot let in air, and without oxygen bacteria and fungi that cause root rot are greatly encouraged. The compost may also become 'sour' and smelly. In these conditions plants usually fail to grow, turn yellow, drop flowers or leaves, and they may begin wilting if the roots decay – this may provoke even more lavish application of water making matters worse! Anything that upsets root function can cause wilting – not only lack of water.

In most homes pot plants will be found standing in saucers to protect furnishings. This is all right provided water is not allowed to remain in the saucer (or any other shallow container that may be used) for any length of time. Ideally pots should not be watered so that excess streams from the drainage hole. If any excess does collect in a saucer or outer container so that it can saturate the potting compost, it should be emptied away when you are sure the compost has taken up all the moisture it can. Overwatering will also wash away valuable soluble plant nutrients, such as nitrates and potassium.

Plants cannot be watered to a timetable and given fixed doses. The amount of water will depend on the type of plant, its size and vigour, the time of year, temperature and light conditions. Aim to keep the potting compost moist and to avoid extremes of dust-dry and waterlogged. Best results are usually achieved when plants are well watered but then allowed to dry out to the slightly moist stage before more water is applied. In winter or when plants are resting or dormant, and also when conditions are cold, far less water should be given. There is greater survival during chilly conditions when plants are kept on the dry side, and watering can often be done at weekly intervals or longer. In summer, however, when it is warm and growth is faster, attention may have to be given more than once a day depending on the plant size.

The best way to judge watering requirements is to feel the compost with your finger. You can also lift a pot and assess its weight. An old method for clay pots was to tap them with a cotton reel on a stick. A high note means that the compost is dry, and a low thud means that it is quite wet. A modern space-age method is to use a moisture meter. This works on electronic principles and there are several types available. They consist of a probe which is inserted into the potting compost. The degree of moisture is indicated by a calibrated dial, usually marked 'dry', 'moist' and 'wet' (Fig. 19).

Fig. 19 A moisture meter takes the guesswork out of watering

House plants are usually watered using a small water can with a narrow spout so that the flow can be easily controlled. All plants can be watered from the top, even those with corms or tubers like cyclamen and gloxinias, provided the water is moderately given, and it is not vital to water from the base by standing the pot in water as frequently suggested. However, in *all* watering *only clean water should be used*. Rainwater collected from roofs should not be employed. It is liable to contain innumerable pests, diseases, and weed seeds. However, it is often supposed that rainwater is beneficial to plants, and it is certainly desirable for those disliking lime or alkaline soils. In this case use rainwater by all means – but collect it in clean containers put out just after rain commences and then store it in clean closed containers. On the other hand there are few cases where pure drinking water from the tap cannot be used. If small quantities of soft water are wanted for a few lime-hating plants you can save the water collected from defrosting the refrigerator. This is almost as good as distilled water regarding purity.

HUMIDITY

Humidity concerns the amount of water vapour in the air. This can vary considerably according to how much water is exposed to the air in the surroundings, and on temperature. We usually notice a high humidity by feeling clammy, with a greater tendency to perspire. A low humidity may cause a feeling of dryness in the nose and throat. In homes where there is central heating or other forms of dry heating like electric fires, the air can become very dry even for human comfort. The majority of plants certainly dislike low humidity and an attempt to increase humidity around them must always be made. The higher the humidity the less frequent is the need for watering, since the plants will lose moisture from their leaves at a slower rate (a process called 'transpiration'). The higher the temperature the higher should be the humidity for most plants, but succulents and other cacti do not have this special preference for humidity. This group is therefore a good choice where it is preferred to keep humidity low – such as a garden room used as a sitting room. The cooler the conditions the less desirable it is for very moist air. In winter the air is best kept on the dry side unless plants are actively growing in congenial warmth. A combination of high humidity with cold encourages fungoid diseases, more especially when ventilation is also poor. You may get trouble from grey mould (see page 40). How much humidity you give your plants consequently depends on the temperature of your rooms, the time of year, and your heating system.

Generally, adequate humidity can be maintained locally around the plants by standing them on a shallow dish or tray containing moist clean grit, sand, or shingle (Fig. 20). For most plants this can be kept

Fig. 20 A humidity tray filled with moist grit or sand will help maintain plant health

moist the year round, but it may be best to let the moisture-holding material go dry over winter. When this method is used there is no need to stand the pots on saucers. Plants placed in outer decorative pots may get sufficient humidity from water rising from the outer pot, but as already pointed out the pot must be raised so that it is not standing in water to cause waterlogging of the compost. Plants in groups usually do well because they create their own humid environment.

In summer most plants benefit from an occasional spray with clean water, but some plants with hairy foliage may be marked by hard tap water. Plants standing in bright sunlight may also become spotted with scorch marks if water droplets on the foliage catch the sun's rays and act like minute 'burning glasses'. Many plants will enjoy being stood out in gentle rain for an hour or so. Stand them on something to keep the pots out of contact with soil, and be careful wind does not blow them over.

The best time for all watering is in the morning. Plants use water best when it is light and when photosynthesis is taking place.

CLEANING PLANT FOLIAGE

A spray with water or a short spell in the rain may keep foliage dust free and looking healthy and attractive. Plant foliage is covered with tiny 'pores' through which pass, in and out, gases like carbon dioxide needed to build organic plant tissues, and waste gases at various times; also waste water in the form of vapour, a flow of which through the plant is vital to carry in nutrients through the roots. This aspect of plant growth is often overlooked, and many house plants may fail because the leaves get dusty and clogged with dirt. Special proprietary products can be obtained for cleaning smooth foliage leaving it with a bright lustre. It is applied with a tuft of cotton wool, and the same method can be used just to wipe the foliage of plants that cannot be sprayed because of immobility or risk to furnishings (Fig. 21). Hairy-leaved plants that collect dust can be brushed gently with a soft camel hair artist's brush.

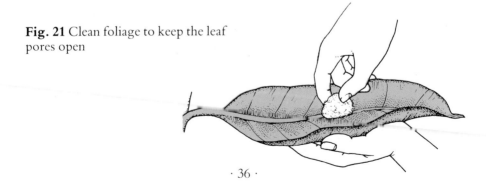

Fig. 21 Clean foliage to keep the leaf pores open

FEEDING PLANTS

When plants are potted in a proper potting compost they will not need feeding for some time. In winter, or when plants are dormant, feeding is not necessary and can indeed be harmful. Like overwatering, overfeeding is a common mistake.

For house plants feeding is best done by using one of the many proprietary products especially designed for them, but general feeds of the soluble type, which also contain trace elements as well as the main plant nutrients, can be used. All these feeds are diluted or dissolved in water before application and contain the essential elements, nitrogen, potassium, and phosphorus, in correctly balanced proportions. Most specially formulated house plant feeds contain some extra nitrogen compared with those for outdoor use, as plants with confined roots need more of this element. Also available are fertilizers in tablet form which can be pressed into the surface of the potting compost and dissolve slowly as the plant is watered normally. A small feed is then given to the plant at every watering. With the exception of these specially made tablets, other feeds in the solid form are best not added to pots (except when making up potting compost). It is easy to overfeed in such circumstances. Fertilizers that are not proper balanced mixtures (called 'straight' fertilizers) such as ammonium sulphate, potassium sulphate, even soot or wood ash, must not be used for pot plants. Also strictly forbidden are crude animal manures of any kind. The *sterilized* proprietary organic concentrates derived from animal sources are, however, all right – provided they are used as the maker instructs. These concentrates are usually best when mixed with potting compost.

FOLIAR FEEDING

It has already been mentioned that leaves have 'pores' (called stomata). These are also able to take in soluble nutrients applied as solutions sprayed onto the foliage. The effect on the plant is usually fast and dramatic, and they respond particularly well to trace elements and magnesium, or vitamins and growth stimulants. Only recently has the effect of certain vitamins on growth been realized. When sprayed on plants they usually have a remarkable effect on growth, leaf, and flower colour. Not all fertilizers are suitable for foliar feeding and some can cause damage. Make sure that you use a specially formulated feed. Some general fertilizers, and most seaweed feeds of the liquid type, can be used for normal and foliar feeding when diluted.

LIGHT, TEMPERATURE, AIR, AND SITE CONDITIONS

Generally it is the extreme of any condition that causes trouble. Plants also often dislike constantly changing conditions, especially temperatures that fluctuate widely over relatively short intervals. By changing temperature slowly over a period of weeks, plants that become used to one level can be acclimatized to another. This mostly applies to plants used to warmth or even from warm countries. The aphelandra, for example, is from Brazil, yet with care it can be gradually introduced to quite cool rooms where it will be pefectly happy if not overwatered.

Most plants like fresh air from time to time and dislike stuffy rooms. Steam may be appreciated and some plants will enjoy a bathroom because of the higher humidity. Fumes from solid fuel fires, coal gas, domestic paraffin heaters, cigarettes, paint or household disinfection – especially bleach fumes (chlorine) which are extremely harmful – can make plants unhappy.

SIMPLE PEST AND DISEASE CONTROL

Because of their protected cultivation, house plants are usually little troubled by pests and diseases. However, an inspection should be made as a routine, looking especially under the foliage where pests and fungi usually first appear. The sooner control is undertaken the easier it is, and there are now several proprietary products that make the job a simple matter. There is also no longer the need to keep innumerable different pesticides, since modern ones have a wide spectrum of control. Now that sterilized potting composts are used, root pests and diseases are quite rare.

The most common pests attacking house plants are aphids (greenfly and sometimes blackfly), which nearly everyone can recognize, whitefly (a tiny greyish-white triangular winged fly), and thrips which produce white patches surrounded by minute black specks on the foliage. All these can be controlled with the new pesticides pirimiphos methyl and permethrin. Useful too for long-lasting action is the new systemic insecticide butoxycarboxin. (Check pesticide container labels for these names.) The systemic group of pesticides are absorbed into a plant's tissues rendering the sap poisonous to the pests. They are now often ingredients of specially impregnated 'pins', made from stiff cardboard, which can be inserted into the plant's compost. There is then a slow release of pesticide for long-term protection.

Systemics are also useful for controlling scale insects, small scale-like

Left: Hedera helix 'Glacier' one of many variegated ivies.
Right: Pteris cretica an easy fern.

creatures that stick fast to the foliage and stems. Small colonies of scale insects can be removed easily by wiping with a small tuft of cotton wool soaked in methylated or surgical spirit. Mealy bugs, which form whitish woolly tufts but are adhesive like scale insects, can be removed similarly.

Thrips can be easily detected if some white paper is placed below and the plant shaken gently. The thrips fall off and will be seen squirming on the white paper quite clearly.

Red spider is a serious pest and may at first go undetected. In the early stages it causes mottling and slight yellowing of foliage. Unchecked it multiplies so that thousands of extremely small mites can be easily seen spinning webbing. At this stage a plant may be so yellowed that it may fail to recover. The pest is not actually a spider – it is a mite. It can be seen, together with tiny round whitish eggs, on plants in the early stages if the underside of leaves are examined with a hand lens. An effective modern pesticide is pirimiphos methyl, but repeated applications may still be necessary. Pesticidal *dusts* are useless. A humid atmosphere will not prevent red spider, but it is discouraging to them. A hot dry place, such as a sunny window sill, is where the pest is most likely to be troublesome.

Moulds and mildews are not usually a nuisance to house plants when the air is generally on the dry side. Grey mould, *Botrytis cinerea*, is the most common and forms a grey to brownish furry mould on plants. It attacks both dead or decaying tissue as well as living, but damaged parts are very susceptible. Removal of fading flowers and damaged or ailing foliage helps to deter the fungus. A cold damp stagnant atmosphere encourages it.

The systemic fungicide Benomyl gives excellent control of grey mould and many other fungi and mildews. Other systemic fungicides are also now available.

To apply these pesticides, a small hand sprayer with a nozzle that will reach under the foliage is necessary (Fig. 22). Always use the pesticides strictly according to label instructions, and obey safety precautions. Do not use kitchen utensils for mixing, do not leave about unused pesticides in vessels normally used for food or drink, or in unlabelled containers, and *keep all pesticides locked away from children.*

ABSENCE AND HOLIDAYS

Obviously the best way to get plants tended during your absence is to get a kind neighbour or friend to take over. If this is not possible water well before you depart and remove plants from windows where they

Fig. 22 A hand sprayer is useful and easy to operate for insecticides

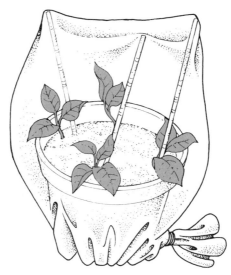

Fig. 23 Polythene tents will help retain humidity while you are on holiday

may be exposed to either hot sun or chill in the winter. Plant windows can be shaded in summer with the product Coolglass used for greenhouses. This should be done from the outside. Although it may look odd for a time to see a completely whitened window, Coolglass has the unique advantage that although perfectly resistant to heavy showers, it can be very easily wiped off with a dry duster.

A simple way to keep plants moist and fresh is to cover them completely with a transparent polythene bag (Fig. 23). Plants will remain in good condition for weeks in many cases. Any other clear glass or plastic cover to keep in moisture can also be used.

Before leaving remove any buds from flowering plants so that the flowers do not fade – and possibly rot – during your absence. A routine spray with a systemic pesticide is also wise.

Pot plants can be stood on a strip of capillary matting (as used for automatic watering in greenhouses) run along the bottom of a bath, and kept moist by allowing a tap to drip – making sure the drainage hole is not obstructed. This method is now often recommended – but it will NOT work if the pots have been well crocked for drainage. There will then be no contact for moisture transfer between the matting and the compost in the pots.

CHAPTER 4

GROWING BULBS

Under the description 'bulbs' are included here corms, tubers, rhizomes, and the like, as well as true bulbs, all collectively known to the botanist as 'storage organs' (Fig. 24). This liberty is taken for the sake of simplicity. They are dealt with in this chapter in three groups: bulbs that have been specially treated to flower early and out of season and called 'prepared' bulbs, spring-flowering bulbs, and summer and autumn flowering types.

Disappointment with bulbs often results through not buying from a reputable supplier. For house plants only the best quality is suitable. They must be of good size, undamaged, firm with no suspicion of sponginess. The performance of a bulb depends on its past history and how well it has been grown before you buy it.

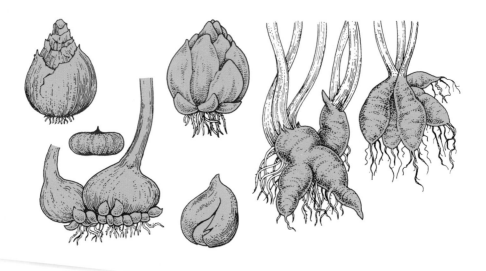

Fig. 24 Different types of storage organ – bulbs, rhizomes and tubers

GENERAL GROWING HINTS

When potting bulbs for house plants there is no need to plant deeply as you would outdoors for weather protection. Often a bulb can be potted with the 'nose' well above the compost. This gives plenty of depth for the roots (Fig. 25).

Bulb fibre is often recommended in books, but this contains no nutrients and if you want to save your bulbs, or grow them on, a proper potting compost (page 90) should be used. Many bulbs begin making new roots and storing nutrients for the next season's flowering when they are making vigorous foliage. This applies to most bulbs after they have finished flowering. At this time do not neglect to continue watering and feeding. This can usually be done until the foliage shows signs of natural deterioration. Then allow the pots gradually to dry, turn out the bulbs, free them from adhering compost, roots and foliage, and store in a dry and airy place. Those bulbs to be kept over winter can be immersed in a box of dry sand and stored in this condition in a frost-free place until it is time to restart them into growth again.

Fig. 25 Bulb with its 'nose' protruding above the compost level

PREPARED BULBS

These are given a special treatment by the suppliers to make them flower early. The bulbs can usually be planted outdoors after they have flowered indoors where, after a year or so, they mostly settle down to normal flowering. They will not flower out of season again.

Hyacinths are very popular and a number of varieties of different colours can be obtained in the prepared form. They are most effective planted three to a bowl and can be flowered for Christmas if bought in autumn and the supplier's instructions are followed (Fig. 26). Roman

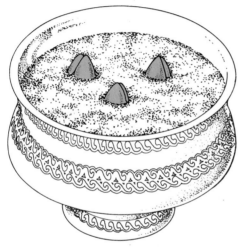

Fig. 26 Groups of bulbs in a single bowl can be very effective

Hyacinths form several spikes of loose white fragrant flowers. After planting keep the containers in the dark until November, then give about 10° C (50° F) and good light. The early hyacinth 'Rosalie', which is rose pink, can be treated similarly.

Prepared daffodils should be plunged (see page 47), removed at the beginning of December, and given full light with a 10–13° C (50–55° F) temperature. It is usually necessary to plant early October. A few varieties can be prepared and include the favourite large-flowered yellow 'Golden Harvest' and the double 'Texas'.

The bunch-flowered narcissi usually grown as prepared bulbs are 'Paperwhite', 'Grand Soleil d'Or' (yellow) and 'Cragford' (white with scarlet cup). They can be grown in a bowl of pebbles placing sufficient pebbles around them to keep them secure. Water should be added to just below the base of the bulbs, and the bowls put in a cool room at about 4–7° C (40–45° F). If in late autumn they are transferred to a room at about 10–13° C (50–55° F), flowers should be out by Christmas.

The few tulip varieties for early flowering are well worth growing, but they should be potted early autumn and plunged as described for spring bulbs (page 47). Before potting remove any adhering broken skin carefully, since this seems to encourage rooting. In early winter remove the pots from the plunge but keep them in the dark in a warm cupboard at about 16° C (60° F) or a few degrees higher if possible – but *not* too warm. When about 5 cm (2 in) of top growth has formed give full light and about 18° C (65° F) on a warm window sill. A very old favourite variety, the non-prepared form of which can also be forced to flower early, is 'Brilliant Star' the bright red.

The giant-flowered hippeastrum hybrids are very spectacular – usually incorrectly called 'amaryllis'. The bulbs are expensive but delightful, usually bearing two stout stems with four enormous flowers on each. Several named varieties are available giving a good colour selection in white and shades of red, pink, and orange. A fairly new introduction is 'Fiery Diamond' which is almost a fluorescent red. The bulbs are grown as described on page 47, but the prepared types must be planted mid-autumn and kept in a warm room *at about* 18° C (65° F) if they are to flower at Christmas.

A few specially treated lilies are now available and very showy. They are of the low growing type bearing handsome heads of several large reflexed flowers. The best effect is obtained by planting three bulbs in an 18 cm (7 in) pot, this time covering the bulbs with about 8 cm (3 in) of compost since they are stem-rooting. Planting should be done in early winter and the pots placed in a sunny window and kept moist, with a temperature of about 18° C (65° F). Flowering is from late winter onwards.

SPRING-FLOWERING BULBS

These include all the garden favourites such as daffodils, and other narcissi, hyacinths, crocus, muscari, tulip varieties and a number of species, galanthus or snowdrops, fritillaria, scilla, and anemone. Worth growing too are many of the lesser known bulbs like alliums (flowering onions), babiana, bulbocodium, chionodoxa, eranthis, erythronium, hermodactylus, leucocoryne, leucojum, puschkinia, tecophilea, and urginea. Many of these can be planted closely in half pots (see page 23) or pans, since they are low-growing and compact, and ideal for a cool sunny window sill.

It is vital to arm yourself with a descriptive catalogue of a specialist bulb nursery (see Appendix). Some named varieties of bulbs are more suited to pot culture than others and *these are always marked in the*

Top left: Maranta leuconeura 'Erythrophylla' Top right: Sansevieria trifasciata laurentii. Bottom left: Begonia rex. Bottom right: Chlorophytum comosum variegatum. Centre: Saintpaulia ionantha.

catalogue. This is most important if you want to force bulbs gently in warmth for early flowers – not all varieties will respond to this, and may fail to flower if an attempt is made.

Pot the bulbs from early to late autumn. Ornamental bowls can be used even if there are no drainage holes – provided watering is done carefully so as not to waterlog. A few lumps of charcoal at the bottom of undrained containers helps keep the compost sweet. Do not overcrowd containers or choose too small a size, or the roots may force the bulb up and out of the compost. If grouping hyacinths select bulbs near the same size so that there is a greater chance of them flowering together.

To promote a vigorous root system containers should be plunged in a box of moist peat after potting; this should be out of doors but covered to prevent rain waterlogging the containers. If you have no garden or outdoor facilities, heap as much moist peat as you can on the planted bowls making sure all is nicely moist, and then cover with a sheet of polythene securing with an elastic band. The covered bowls can then be stood on an outside window sill or balcony, or anywhere where it is quite cool. At this stage warmth will prove disastrous by forcing top growth before the roots have grown.

After potting it is usually about 6 to 8 weeks before top growth appears. At this stage all covering should be removed and the containers stood in a cool shady place for about a week. Thereafter, gradually introduce the containers to full light to avoid the foliage becoming pale and weak.

When potting large bulbs like hyacinths and narcissi leave the nose protruding from the compost. While the pots are in the plunge, or under the heaped peat cover, check from time to time to see that the peat is moist.

Although cold at this stage is important, freezing is best avoided since it can cause root damage and stunting. The tall flowering spring bulbs will usually need a few split canes around the foliage and inconspicuous cotton thread to keep the foliage tidy. Narcissi and the taller tulips are best given pots rather than bowls. The short double tulips make particularly neat and showy displays in bowls.

SUMMER-, AUTUMN-, AND SOME WINTER-FLOWERING BULBS

These are important flowering house plants suiting a variety of situations, and they are mostly easy to grow. The following are some particular favourites described in alphabetical order:

Achimenes

Species and named varieties with a wide range of lovely flower colours can be bought from specialists. Pot the catkin-like tubercules in late winter, using half pots or hanging baskets for trailing types. Just cover with compost. Best temperature about 15–18° C (60–65° F). Give slightly shaded place and support if necessary with twiggy sticks unless wanted to trail.

Begonia

Tuberous begonias have several flower types – large flowered, multiflora, and pendant for baskets. Pot in early spring just setting the tubers level with the compost surface, placing them concave or flat side uppermost. Give large flowered or multiflora types 13 cm (5 in) pots. Set several of the pendant type around the edge of a basket or other hanging container. Remove female flowers (those with seed pod attached) from giant-flowered types as they form – usually one each side of the double male flower. This will improve bloom quality and plant vigour. Give shaded situation. Best temperature about 13° C (55° F).

Caladium

These plants are grown from tubers usually sold as named hybrids. The foliage is impressively beautiful, the large heart-shaped leaves being flushed, marbled and speckled, with bright colours, often having contrasting veins and borders.

The tubers can be started into growth in moist peat during early spring, but a temperature of about 24° C (75° F) will be needed. When growth begins, pot the tubers in a pot just large enough to take them – the size often varies considerably. From then on the plants will grow quickly provided a warm place can be found and they are kept moist. To get the best leaf coloration choose somewhere as bright as possible, but shaded from direct sunshine. Spray the foliage with a fine mist of soft water from time to time during summer and give liquid feeds.

In autumn when the foliage deteriorates, let the pots almost dry out – but not quite. They can be stored over winter where the temperature does not fall below about 13° C (55° F) and started into growth again the following spring.

Often caladiums are bought already in leaf from a florist. This is a good way to choose leaf colours and markings. In countries where the climate is warm, caladiums are very easy. Where it's chilly, there is often trouble from leaf deterioration.

Colchicum (autumn crocus)

Large corms of varieties such as 'Lilac Wonder', 'The Giant', and 'Water Lily', all lilac to mauve in colour, can be flowered by just sitting them on a saucer of dry sand placed on a window sill. No soil or water is necessary, but after flowering they should be planted in a garden if possible. Purchase for starting into growth late summer to early autumn. Flowering is at various times during autumn. Bright cool window sill.

Cyclamen

This is one of the most popular house plants given as a present when beginning to bloom. It is not unusual for such plants to wilt and die owing to the sudden change from greenhouse to room conditions.

The easiest and most inexpensive way to grow your own is to start from corms. Obtain these from about mid- to late-summer and give each a 13 cm (5 in) pot. See that the corms are planted with any slight depression they may have upwards and the convex side downwards, and leave a third of the corm portruding above the compost surface. The pots can be kept outside in a shady place during the summer and watered just sufficiently to maintain a moist compost. When the corms begin to grow water can be given more generously. In early autumn the plants can be brought indoors and put on a bright window sill, but shaded from direct sunshine. Try to maintain a temperature of about 10° C (50° F) without too much fluctuation. If you want the main show of flowers to be from winter to spring, remove any early buds that may form.

Eucomis bicolor (pineapple flower)

Not well known but easy. An attractive spike of greenish lilac flowers capped with a tuft of foliage reminiscent of the pineapple rises from a rosette of foliage from mid- to late summer. The flower, however, sometimes has an offensive smell! Give the large bulbs a 13 cm (5 in) pot each leaving the nose well protruding. Pot early spring. Bulb is almost hardy. Slight shade in summer. Pink shades and white are recently introduced colours and very attractive.

Gloriosa rothschildiana (gloriosa lily)

This lovely plant with red and yellow flowers like reflexed lilies is much easier to grow than supposed. It can be allowed to climb when it will reach about 120 cm (4 ft), or put in a hanging container to trail. The leaves have tendrils for climbing. Pot the elongated tubers from mid- to late-spring giving a temperature of about 16° C (60° F). An 18 cm (7 in) pot is sufficient. Flowers usually come from summer to autumn. Slight shade, good humidity.

   A special method of potting should be adopted. The thick round end of the tuber is the point where new stem and root growth begins. This should therefore be potted centrally in the pot and just covered with compost. The remainder of the tuber can rest along the surface and even project over the pot rim if there's insufficient room. As the plant grows the *original* tuber *shrivels*, and new ones (usually two) form downwards into the compost of the pot. Let the pots go dry over winter and store frost-free. Turn them out and repot the new tubers as described when it's starting time again.

Gloxinia

If potted early spring, one tuber to each 13 cm (5 m) pot, numerous large showy trumpet flowers appear late summer to autumn. Attractive velvety foliage. Before potting immerse tubers in moist peat in a warm place. Inspect from time to time to check for shooting. It is then easy to pot the right way up which may not be obvious before shoots appear. About 16° C (60° F) is ideal. Shade and good humidity.

Haemanthus multiflorus

A remarkable flower like an enormous crimson dandelion clock borne on a strong stem above a rosette of foliage. Pot the large bulbs with the nose exposed in spring. Water sparingly until growth is seen. Flowers late summer to autumn. Temperature about 10–16° C (50–60° F), slight shade. If the winter temperature is low, keep the bulbs almost dry. In warmth they continue to grow.

Hippeastrum (commonly incorrectly called 'amaryllis')

Prepared bulbs have been discussed on page 44. Pot ordinary bulbs in early spring giving 18 cm (7 in) pot to each and leaving at least two-thirds of the bulb protruding above the compost. Sometimes the flowers are produced before the foliage and before rooting has taken place – be careful that the plant does not fall over if it is moved about. Roots begin to grow with the foliage and water can then be freely given. Flowers should appear from summer to autumn.

   In winter do not dry off (as frequently recommended). Keep at about 7° C (45° F) and give only sufficient water to maintain foliage. The following year flowers should come with the foliage present and be more numerous and of better quality. In its natural home this bulb is evergreen. Slight shade. About 13–16° C (55–60° F) from potting to autumn.

Hymenocallis calathina (Peruvian daffodil)

In catalogues this is often listed as 'Ismene'. Several large fragrant white flowers, like spidery daffodils, are borne on a tall strong stem. If the large bulbs are potted as for hippeastrum in spring, flowers come in summer.

Buy bulbs as large as possible or they may not be of flowering size. Slight shade. Temperature about 10–16° C (50–60° F). Leave bulbs in their pots and keep almost dry during winter.

Lilium

There are numerous species and spectacular hybrids. Most can be grown in pots, the taller kinds being good for porches or a bright hallway. Some are stem-rooting and must be potted well down and not with nose exposed. If roots are seen to form at the base of the stems, they should be just covered by the addition of a little extra fresh potting compost. A compost based on leafmould gives good results.

Pot from autumn to spring. Flowering occurs from summer to autumn according to variety and species.

Consult a grower's catalogue for descriptions of the numerous hybrids and for information on which are stem-rooting. Use 15–20 cm (6–8 in) pots, and *plunge* as for spring–flowering bulbs (page 47). Temperature 7–13° C (45–55° F), avoid too much warmth. Slight shade.

Nerine (Guernsey lily)

For the house choose the named hybrids. These must be potted in late summer leaving the nose well exposed, one bulb per 13 cm (5 in) pot. At first put the pots outdoors on a sunny window sill or stand on a paved area. Give no water until growth commences, then water generously. Transfer pots to an indoor window sill in autumn. Large umbels of flowers in beautiful colours and with a glistening sheen are produced up until early winter. Leave bulbs in their pots dry over winter. Do not repot for several years.

Polyanthus tuberosa (tuberose)

Foliage is often untidy, but the strongly scented white spikes of flowers are good for cutting. Best planted three to an 18 cm (7 in) pot. If a temperature of about 13–16° C (55–60° F) is available, the bulbs can be brought into flower at almost any time. After flowering expose to as much sun as possible, otherwise the bulbs may fail to flower the following year. The bulbs are imported and, in the UK, rarely flower well a second time – if at all.

Sauromatum venosum (monarch of the east, voodoo lily)
A curiosity, to grow like colchicum without soil or water at first. A strange short-lived arum-like 'flower' is produced which may smell horrid. After this performance, pot the tuber. It will then produce a tall spotted stem bearing handsome palm-like foliage at the top and is really then quite decorative. Buy the largest tubers you can get. Not fussy about position or temperature, within reason.

Smithiantha (temple bells)
Buy modern named varieties which have glorious velvety foliage in unusual shades of green, often with metallic sheen, and columns of flowers in lovely colours. Pot the rhizomes late winter, one to a 13 cm (5 in) pot or three to an 18 cm (7 in). Just cover with compost, If a warm window sill is not available leave potting until early spring. Flowering is from summer to autumn depending on potting time. Best temperature is about 13–16° C (55–60° F). Shade well during summer. Good humidity. Keep in the pots and allow to go dry during the rest period.

Sprekelia formosissima (Jacobean lily, Aztec lily)
Buy large bulbs and pot as for hippeastrum in early spring in 13 cm (5 in) pots. The strange flower comes from summer onwards depending on potting time. It has thin petals in deep crimson, and usually appears before the foliage. Keep the bulbs dry in their pots during the rest period. Temperature about 13° C (55° F), shade.

Vallota speciosa (Scarborough lily)
Buy large bulbs and pot like hippeastrum in late summer. Heads of large impressive flowers in bright orange-red shades are produced on strong stems in autumn, several to each stem. Treatment is as for hippeastrum.

Veltheimia capensis
Pot the large bulbs, one to each 13 cm (5 in) pot, in autumn. The bulbs produce a rosette of attractive foliage. From this rises a tall stem with a flower reminiscent of red hot poker of the outdoor garden (*Kniphofia*), but the colours are usually pale shades of pink and not very showy. However, it is useful for it flowers from early winter onwards. Not fussy about temperature or position within reason. If the flower colours could be improved this would be a highly desirable house plant.

CHAPTER 5

EASY HOUSE PLANTS FROM SEED

In many households experiments are made at growing plants from seeds on window sills. The seeds are often fruit pips and 'stones' and the resulting plants may be anything but decorative. Even if grown on to maturity many fruits from pips will not come true to type if the seed was taken from commercial fruit which is usually of grafted origin. In this chapter some very decorative plants you can quickly grow from seed are described.

EQUIPMENT NEEDED

You will need one or more plastic seed trays, the small size being better if only a few sowings are to be made (Fig. 27). If you can obtain these with a clear plastic cover or dome to fit, this will be additionally useful. Alternatively get some pieces of window glass cut to cover the trays, or find some plastic bags that they will slip into. The plastic must be clear and polythene is quite suitable. A few small pots with dome covers may be useful.

Most garden shops sell small bags of sowing and cutting compost, which are in fact intended for window sill gardeners. One of these is enough to sow very many seeds, and it is essential to your success. DO NOT USE SOIL TAKEN FROM OUTDOORS.

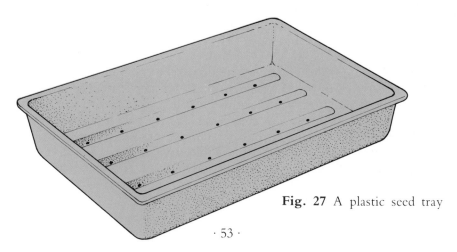

Fig. 27 A plastic seed tray

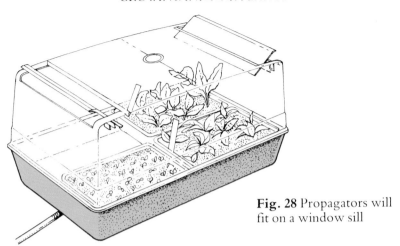

Fig. 28 Propagators will fit on a window sill

Most house plant seeds need reasonable warmth for germination. On a window sill of a moderately warm room with temperatures ranging between about 7–21° C (55–70° F) no extra warmth should be necessary for germination of the following seeds. However, you can now buy small seed tray electric warming plates which take one or two seed trays (Fig. 28). This piece of equipment could be a great help. With care and common sense warmth from a radiator may be used, but the danger is in overheating which will completely ruin the seeds.

TECHNIQUE

Buy best quality seed from specialist firms (see Appendix). Choose F_1 hybrid varieties when possible, since these are superior in vigour; compact forms are best for pots. Sow as soon as possible after you receive the seed. Early spring is usually the best time.

Make sure the seed compost is moist before sowing and kept constantly moist all the time. Moist does not mean waterlogged. It is vital that the compost does not dry out during germination or there may be complete failure.

Do not sow deeply. Fine seed should not be covered at all. A rough guide is to cover the seed with about its own depth of seed compost. Sow thinly. There is no need to sow a whole packet or you may get far more seedlings than you can cope with. In any case it is wise to save some seed in the event of the first failing, or for a supply of later flowering or maturing plants. If possible sow large seeds individually with the fingers or a pair of tweezers so that you can space them well (Fig. 29). Very fine seed can be mixed with dry silver sand for more even distribution.

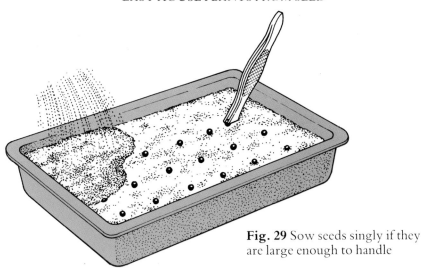

Fig. 29 Sow seeds singly if they are large enough to handle

After sowing cover the seed tray with a sheet of white paper then with a sheet of glass. Trays fitted with a plastic cover should also first be covered with paper so that it does not touch the compost surface (Fig. 30). The same applies to trays slipped in polythene bags. The idea of the paper is to stop condensation dripping onto the seed compost causing waterlogging. Seeds must have moisture *and air* to germinate. Waterlogging will suffocate them.

Inspect the seed trays every day, and if necessary apply more water with a hand sprayer that delivers a fine mist. As soon as germination is seen remove all covers, but if you have to be away for any length of time leave the transparent cover on for a time. Expose the seedlings to good light – but not direct sunshine.

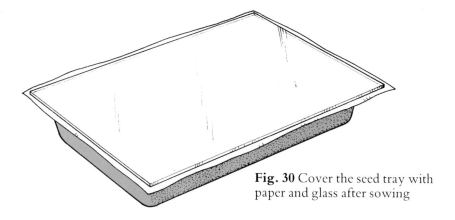

Fig. 30 Cover the seed tray with paper and glass after sowing

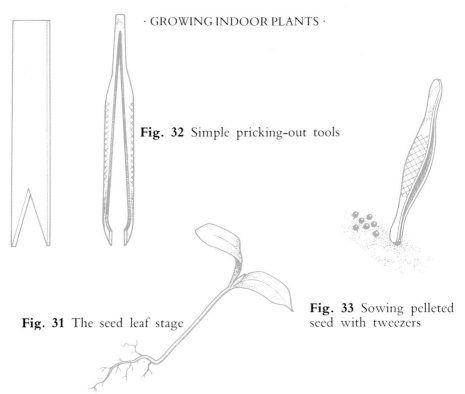

Fig. 32 Simple pricking-out tools

Fig. 31 The seed leaf stage

Fig. 33 Sowing pelleted seed with tweezers

As soon as they are large enough to handle transfer them carefully to individual small pots of potting compost (see page 29). Ideally this should be done at the seed leaf stage and before the first true leaves characteristic of the plant have developed (Fig. 31). A pair of finely tipped tweezers is a useful tool for transferring the seedlings, or a piece of flat thin wood or plastic with a 'V' notch cut in the end. When pricking out with tweezers, DO NOT use them to *grasp* stems or leaves. Use the points as a tiny 'fork' to lift the roots, adjusting distance apart of the points to suit seedling size (Fig. 32).

Large seeds can often be sown in their first pots individually and left to grow until they need potting on. In this case use a potting compost for sowing. Some seed can be obtained in the pelleted form to make handling easier (Fig. 33). These can also be sown, say a couple to each small pot, thinning to leave one sturdy seedling after germination. The technique of thinning – pulling out unwanted seedlings leaving only one or a group to grow on – may also be useful instead of pricking out. Much depends on the cost and quantity of the seed.

Abutilon hybrids (flowering maple)

These are excellent flowering house plants with maple like foliage. They are perennial, often flowering in winter, but they will flower the first year from seed sown in spring. They may grow very tall but can be cut back to induce branching growth. The flowers have shades of pink, red and yellow, and are attractively veined. Pot on to a final 13 cm (5 in) pot for flowering. Happy in good light and frost-free conditions. A recommended variety is 'Bella'.

Acacia dealbata (mimosa)
This is easy and makes an attractive foliage plant in the young stage. However, flowers are unlikely unless you can grow it to considerable size in a conservatory. It is hardy in parts of the south and west outdoors.

Asparagus (so called 'asparagus ferns')
Asparagus is not a fern. Several species are splendid house plants and surplus foliage can be cut to go with vase flowers. Most popular is *A. sprengeri* often used in hanging containers because of its trailing tendency. It can however be kept upright with supports. *A. plumosus* has extremely fine needle foliage, is erect, and has the habit of a cedar tree. Delightful with erect compact clumps of foliage, but slow growing, is *A. meyersii*. Mature plants will also bear a good crop of red berries. All grow well in frost-free conditions. A 13 cm (5 in) pot is generally suitable.

Begonias
These are best sown as early in the year as possible since they are slow growers at first. The fibrous sorts used for garden bedding make pleasing pot plants often flowering well during the winter on a sunny window sill. There are several varieties with bronze or variegated foliage, or extra large flowers, specially good for pots. Tuberous kinds, more especially the multiflora doubles, can also be grown quite easily from seed and will flower the first year if sown early. A particularly striking species, with many large beautiful scarlet single flowers, is *B. bertinii. B rex,* the well known foliage begonia, can be grown from seed, but it's not easy. Use 9–13 cm (3½–5 in) pots, and give bright position.

Browallia speciosa
This is a perennial, flowering the first year if sown early, and also useful for winter flowers. The blooms are blue and cup-shaped. For winter flowering sowing can be made during summer. In chilly places winter-saved plants may deteriorate and not flower. They can however be saved and cut back in spring when they will flower in autumn. Use

Pilea 'Moon Valley' is another beautiful Pilea. Grow as for the better known *P. cadierei* or Aluminium Plant.

Primula obconica has flowers in delightfully showy colours, but its leaves may cause skin irritation.

13 cm (5 in) pots. A recently introduced very dwarf and compact form is the 'Troll' strain also available in white.

Calceolarias and cinerarias

These are among the most showy flowering pot plants, but have to be discarded after the blooms have faded and raised freshly from seed each year. Calceolarias have pouch-shaped flowers in profusion, exotically coloured and spotted in bright shades of yellow and red. Cinerarias have masses of daisy-like blooms often in vivid and dramatic colours sometimes zoned with white. Both have large and small multiflora forms, but for use as house plants it is important to choose compact varieties from the seed catalogues. There are magnificent giant exhibition forms, but these are really better suited to a greenhouse. A particularly good calceolaria is the F_1 hybrid 'Glorious Formula'. This is an exceptionally neat plant and is remarkably quick flowering. It will bloom well in only 9 cm (3½ in) pots. Also ideal window sill cinerarias are the new varieties 'Cindy' and 'Amigo'.

Seed of both calceolarias and cinerarias can be sown from late spring to early summer to give plants flowering from late autumn to spring. The large-flowered exhibition forms generally flower later than

Pelargonium 'Ringo Salmon' one of many superb F₁ hybrid 'geraniums' you can now grow easily from seed.

Salpiglossis is extremely exotic looking, but easy to grow from F hybrid seed.

multiflora and compact varieties. For Christmas display, sow early.

No artificial warmth is needed for seed germination. Pot on to 9 cm (3½ in) pots for small varieties to at least 13 cm (5 in) pots for the larger forms. Keep the plants cool and shaded at all times. They are very prone to wilt if exposed to direct sunlight and warmth. Both should be checked frequently for the presence of aphids which seem to be a particular problem of these plants. Routine systemic insecticide treatment is wise.

Capsicums and solanums

These are quite different species, but of the same plant family and can be grown similarly. Capsicums are much easier to grow than solanums, which are usually known as winter cherry. Winter cherry must be sown as early as possible and when in flower in summer put on an outdoor window sill for flower pollination by insects. Or you can spray from time to time with a mist of water. A generally unknown fact is that the berries are frequently poisonous. The fruits of capsicums are usually more elongated than winter cherry, often very much so. They form easily and with freedom and sowing can be left until spring, or even later if you don't want berries until Christmas. The fruits may be very 'hot' to taste, but are not poisonous. There are many forms with, like winter cherry, orange, yellow, or scarlet fruits. These may be borne upright or pointing down. 'Red Fangs' and 'Fips' are varieties with elongated fruits. There are also some with variegated foliage. Bright position. A 9–13 cm (3½ –5 in) pot. A feed with Epsom salts, sprinkled over the compost surface, helps to counteract magnesium deficiency to which these species are sometimes prone.

Celosia (cockscomb)
There are two types of celosia, the 'crested' and the 'plumed'. The former has strange flower heads shaped like a cock's comb, and the latter feathery plumes. The colours usually embrace a wide range of reds and yellows. Celosia is long lasting, but is an annual and must be discarded after the show is over.

When choosing varieties from the seed catalogues, look for the dwarf forms which make neat pot plants. Sow late winter to early spring and pot on to 9 cm (3½ in) pots which are generally large enough. The plants like a bright window position to develop the best colours.

Coleus (flame nettle)
Very popular with wonderful selection of leaf colours. It is best raised as an annual since plants often deteriorate over winter. Many varieties with fancy leaf shapes are also now available. To select colours for a mixed packet of seed the seedlings can be grown at first in seed trays. When the leaves have developed their colours the less interesting seedlings can be thrown out and the others potted. 'Carefree' is a new F_1 hybrid with many unusual colours. A delightful new miniature variety for the window sill, growing only about 12½ cm (5 in) high, is 'Mini-Coral'.

Cuphea ignea (Mexican cigar plant)
This is a delightful, neat plant, with masses of small tubular scarlet flowers with black tip. It is remarkable for fast flowering. Best grown as annual. Sunny position. 9 cm (3½ in) pots.

Exacum affine
This species should have a strong spicy fragrance to the small blue flowers, but recent attempts to increase flower size and compactness have often lost the scent in the process. Be sure to obtain a seed strain that still retains the fragrance, such as 'Suttons Starlight Fragrance' which is also neat growing. Grow several seedlings to each 13 cm (5 in) pot. Shade and good humidity. Autumn flowers if sown in spring.

Freesia

Sow a good strain of seed in mid-winter, about seven seeds to each 13 cm (5 in) pot. Give a temperature of about 13° C (60° F). Support foliage with sticks and cottons. Give bright position. Flowers can be expected from summer onwards. Plants will form corms which should be ripened before storing (page 43) by spreading in the sun.

Grevillea robusta (Australian silky oak)

In its early stages this makes an impressive foliage plant with large 'ferny' leaves. It will, however, eventually grow to a considerable size and may have to be discarded in favour of younger plants through lack of space. Cutting back will encourage branching and helps to keep plants compact. Use a lime-free potting compost. Minimum winter temperature about 7–10° C (45–50° F), otherwise leaves may be lost. Good light 13–18 cm (5–7 in) pots, or bigger for large specimens.

Hypoestes sanguinolenta (polka dot plant)

This is very easy to raise from seed and plants of useful size develop the same year as sowing if this is done early. The leaves are a dark olive green freely variegated with many small bright pink spots, giving the plant a striking and very characteristic appearance. Although a charming foliage plant it has a tendency to become leggy and untidy with age. This can be checked to some extent by cutting back whenever possible to encourage as much basal branching growth as possible. Give a position of good light avoiding direct sunlight. Plants often survive quite chilly conditions in winter, but young specimens are usually the most attractive and it is easy to raise fresh stock from seed each year. A specially recommended new variety with rich colouring, and less tendency to straggle, is 'Pink Splash'.

Impatiens (busy lizzie)

This popular plant is quick flowering from seed and numerous fine varieties which are free flowering, compact, and even with variegated foliage, can be obtained, also F₁ hybrids. Some have bicoloured flowers in white and shades of red, orange, and pink. Far better plants are obtained easily from seed than from obscure cuttings from friends. 9–13 cm (3½–5 in) pots, good light or slight shade. Double-flowered varieties have recently been introduced but, so far, seem to be less compact and less free flowering.

Ipomoea tricolor (morning glory)

This beautiful annual climber is often successful in a sunny window or porch. It can be trained up bamboo canes, or any suitable support, but can grow to a considerable size and may have to be restricted. Several fancy-coloured varieties in shades of pink and red can be obtained, but the loveliest is still the old fashioned vivid blue form 'Heavenly Blue'. The convolvulus blooms are very large, last only from morning to early afternoon, but are freely produced over several months. 13–18 cm (5–7 in) pots, three seedlings to each for the larger size, depending on space available.

Jacaranda mimosaefolia

Similar to *Grevillea robusta* but with more graceful and delicately structured foliage. A very beautiful foliage plant. It does not need an acid compost like grevillea, but otherwise culture is the same.

Lobelia tenuoir

Similar to garden edging lobelia, but with much more exotic appearance and large beautiful blue flowers in great profusion. Best grown as several seedlings in half pots with twiggy sticks for support. Best sown in spring, since it does not like chill. Good humidity and slight shade. Flowers from summer to autumn.

Mimosa pudica (sensitive plant)

One of the most remarkable curiosities of the vegetable kingdom. The mimosa-like leaves are sensitive to touch and fold up in a most dramatic manner. Amusing to children of all ages! Plants are perennial, but young plants are the most sensitive. A few pinkish mimosa-like flowers are produced, but are of no importance. 9 cm (3½ in) pots for young plants. Bright position.

Pelargoniums ('geranium')

The so-called 'geraniums' were at one time not a practical proposition from seed. The recent introduction of F_1 hybrid seed, which yields fine quality flowers a few months after sowing, has changed this. You will find an exciting selection of named F_1 seed described in the catalogues of the leading seed firms, covering a wide spectrum of glorious colours. They mostly have the habit of the well-known zonal pelargonium group, but there are also some very new forms. For examples, 'Startel' has starry florets and a powerful leaf scent, 'Red Fountains' has a cascading habit, and 'Summer Showers' is the first *ivy* type to be offered as seed and is ideal for hanging baskets or display on pedestals.

In all cases, whatever the 'geranium' type, never be afraid to cut back severely if plants get leggy or untidy. Give good light, water very sparingly in winter and keep frost-free. Sow seed individually, and germinate at about 21° C (70° F). Generally useful pot size for flowering is 13 cm (5 in).

Primula

Several primulas are sold as house plants, but some like *P. malacoides* (fairy primula) and *P. sinensis* (Chinese primula) are short-lived. *P. obconica* (poison primrose) is, however, remarkable for lasting many years and often flowering generously almost the year round. The disadvantage with this species is that it shares with *P. sinensis* the characteristic of causing a painful or itchy skin rash in those people allergic to the leaf hair secretion. There is unfortunately no way of

Ficus elastica doescheri (*left*) and *Euphorbia pulcherrima* or poinsettia (*right*) with chlorophytum, Saintpaulia and *Begonia rex*.

overcoming this and if a rash is noticed it is best to have nothing to do with the plants.

P. obconica, like most primulas, prefers an acid compost. Plants can be kept in 13 cm (5 in) pots for a long time. Keep the compost moist, give liquid feeds when active growth is being made, and choose a place of cool shade in summer. Modern varieties have large showy flower clusters in salmon pink, red, purple, mauve, and blue shades, also white. Good plants can be raised from seed if desired. Sowing can be made from early spring to mid-summer to produce plants flowering from winter to spring.

P. malacoides can also be raised easily from seed if preferred, but it is an annual and must be discarded after flowering. It has the advantage of not causing skin dermatitis. It is also a charming dainty primula bearing stems carrying whorls of flowers one above the other. 9 cm (3½ in) pots are generally large enough for flowering specimens. Both vivid and pastel colour shades are obtainable, but when growing from seed a strain giving a mixture of colours is pleasing.

Ricinus communis (castor oil plant)

This is a very easy plant to grow from the large bean-like seed which can be sown, one to a 9 cm (3½ in) pot, on a warm window sill in early spring. Special varieties with reddish-purple leaf colour can be selected from seed catalogues. Pot on to 13 cm (5 in) pots or larger. This plant is particularly useful for a bright sunny window, but to display its full beauty needs plenty of space by autumn, and by that time a larger pot.

Although perennial, this plant is really best grown as an annual. It is very fast growing and will make a handsome specimen very quickly the first year. The seeds are poisonous, and since they are attractively marked, should not be allowed to fall into the hands of children who may swallow them. Two fine new varieties, with rich red-bronze foliage and eye-catching vermilion spiky seed capsules, are 'Impala' and 'Mizuma' which can be specially recommended for pots.

Saintpaulia (African violet)

The introduction of F_1 hybrids has made this plant a practical proposition to raise from seed. Usually available are 'Blue Fairy Tale' and 'Pink Fairy Tale'. The plants are, however, certainly not a 'fairy tale'. They are very real and beautiful. The colours are rich and the flowers large and single, and borne very freely even on young plants. A splendid new variety giving a wide range of colours is 'Velvet Gems'. An early sowing will give an abundance of plants flowering from early autumn onwards. Saintpaulias do well grown under artificial light (see page 89). 9 cm (3½ in) pots for young flowering plants. Reasonable warmth, shade, and humidity. Best winter minimum about 13° C (55° F).

Salpiglossis

The best forms to grow on a sunny window sill are the F_1 hybrids 'Splash' and 'Ingrid' which are outstandingly more neat and free-flowering than the older varieties. Grow one or three seedlings to each 13 cm (5 in) pot and give a split cane for support. When a few inches tall, snip the top off the seedlings to induce branching. Many exquisite trumpet-shaped flowers are produced from early summer onwards. There are many shades of blue, red, and yellow, with exotic veining in gold. A thrilling and easy flower to grow as an annual, but be sure to get a variety recommended here. It is more compact and superior to all others.

Schizanthus (butterfly flower)

Another delightful annual with several vastly improved hybrids. For the home the dwarf variety 'Hit Parade' is one of the best. It is very compact but has the flower size and remarkable colour range to be found in the tall giant forms. Plant several seedlings to each 13 cm (5 in) pot. The dainty ferny foliage and innumerable gaily marked and coloured flowers make this an important window sill plant. Staggered sowing will prolong the time you can enjoy this flower.

Thunbergia alata (black-eyed Susan)

An exciting little climber with striking orange flowers with jet black eye. It flowers as a small seedling and any pale colours or eye-less specimens can be thrown out if you wish. A packet of seed usually yields some of these. One to three seedlings can be put to each 13 cm (5 in) pot and trained up a fan of canes. An exceptionally large flowered new variety is 'Susie'. Watch out for red spider attack to which this plant is very prone. Slight shade prevents bleaching of the flowers. The plant is actually perennial, although classed as an annual. It is certainly best discarded at the end of the year.

Torenia fournieri (wishbone flower)

A charming annual with unusually structured yellow-throated blue flowers. Best grown as several seedlings to each 13 cm (5 in) pot. Can also be grown in hanging baskets or containers, otherwise supported with twiggy sticks to keep upright. Needs congenial temperature and best sown not earlier than spring. Good humidity, shade.

CHAPTER 6

EASY PLANTS FOR FOLIAGE AND FLOWERS

In this chapter are described a range of easy plants that can be bought from most garden centres, florist shops, or house plant nurseries. What the author considers difficult plants have been omitted, also those needing considerable warmth and humidity. Provided the simple instructions and notes are given consideration, most people should have success with the following.

Aphelandra squarrosa louisae (zebra plant)
A striking plant, the glossy leaves boldly veined in cream and strange angular yellow flowers borne by mature plants. Although from Brazil, this plant can be gradually acclimatized to quite cool rooms. Best bought during summer months. Water well in summer but very sparingly in winter. 13 cm (5 in) pot. Winter minimum temperature about 7–10° C (45–58° F).

Aspidistra elatior (cast iron plant)
Well known for resistance to ill-treatment but nowadays often despised. However, a well-grown plant with a foliage kept shiny with a modern leaf-shine product can be a handsome sight. The variegated form with cream stripes is especially attractive.

Azalea japonica
Hardy azaleas must not be confused with the tender *A. indica* and similar types sold by florists. These have been forced into bloom in warm greenhouses. Buy hardy dwarf types from a garden centre. Acid compost, cool airy conditions. Good for an open porch. Not suitable for warm rooms. Stand out in rain when possible.

Begonias for foliage
There are many species and named hybrids of begonias grown for their beautiful foliage, but none is suited to chilly conditions. They also like good humidity and usually shade. Often they bear attractive clusters of white, pink, or red flowers. *B. rex* with silvery marked spade-shaped leaves often flushed with pink or purple, is well known but not the

easiest. *B. corallinia* is easier, but tall growing. It has similar shaped leaves with white above and wine red below. Large clusters of pink flowers hang from the stems. Similar but with red flowers and red-margined foliage is *B. coccinea*, and 'President Canot' is a fine hybrid. With especially striking foliage is *B masoniana* (the iron cross begonia) with a bold dark iron cross mark on the leaves. 'Chantilly Lace', a hybrid with lace-like markings around the leaf margins, and 'St Albans Grey' with leaves grey-green above the reddish underneath. Most foliage begonias can be propagated from leaf cuttings.

Beloperone guttata (shrimp plant)
Grown for its strange shrimp-shaped and coloured bracts which develop the best tints *exposed to full sunlight*. If plants deteriorate in winter cut them back in spring. Minimum temperature about 7° C (45° F). About 13 cm (5 in) pots.

Bromeliads (urn plants)
Although related to the pineapple, most do not need high temperatures. Those with smooth-edged leaves usually grow naturally above ground on the bark of trees and where moss has collected. Those with barbed leaves are ground dwellers. Both like an open mossy compost containing also peat, leafmould, and grit. Foliage is often richly coloured or marked, but the plainer bromeliads usually have strange, spectacular flowers. Most have a central hollow in the rosette of foliage called the 'urn' and this can be kept filled with water. Many species can now be obtained, and the catalogue of a specialist grower should be consulted. A plant will flower only once but produces new plantlets around the base. These should be detached and potted on to continue the species. Generally they like good humidity and winter light, shade in summer, and a winter minimum temperature of about 10° C (50° F).

Cacti and other succulents
There are a tremendous number and again specialist catalogues and books should be consulted but many can be grown easily from seed. Most will stand long periods of neglect – but they do need reasonable watering in summer for best results. Many will produce quite showy flowers. Epiphyllums are exceptionally showy. Good house plants for flowers too are kalanchoe, of which there are several named hybrids, *Schlumbergera* × *buckleyi* (Christmas cactus), *S. truncata* (crab cactus, also winter flowering), *Rhipsalidopsis gaertneri* (Easter cactus), a number of *Crassula* species, *Lithops* (living stones), *Aloe* species, *Echinocereus* species, *Rebutia* species, *Parodia* species, *Mammillaria* species, and the

popular gherkin cactus, *Chamaecereus silvestrii*. These are just a few that flower freely. Most like a sunny window sill, and a potting compost well drained by the addition of washed grit. Minimum winter temperature about 7° C (45° F).

Campanula isophylla

An old favourite basket campanula for hanging containers or wall pots. There are both blue and white forms. Leaf variegation often occurs spontaneously, but the flower size sometimes then deteriorates. Slight shade, winter minimum about 7° C (45° F). Flowers mid-summer to autumn.

Chlorophytum elatum *syn. C. capense* (spider plant)

An attractive easy foliage plant with long narrow green foliage striped creamy-white. It produces arching stems carrying small plants at their ends. These will root if layered (see page xx). Long stems of small creamy flowers are also produced, but these are not showy. A good plant for wall pots or hanging containers and pedestals. Good light, temperature minimum 7° C (45° F) 13 cm (5 in) pots or larger.

Chrysanthemum

Nearly all chrysanthemums sold by florists as house plants have been specially treated by the nursery to form dwarf plants flowering out of season. If you have no outdoor garden it is not usually worth saving the plants after they have flowered, since they will grow very much taller if potted on. They will also flower during their natural period from about late summer to autumn. Chrysanthemums will last a remarkably long time in flower if given a cool airy room and a bright position.

Charm chrysanthemums, with masses of small single flowers in a wide colour range, can be grown from seed sown in late winter. The seedlings and plants should be stopped several times during growth to promote bushiness and compact plants. They will flower in 13–18 cm (5–7 in) pots in autumn.

Citrus mitis (calamondin orange)

This is one of the best citrus for the home since it flowers and bears small fruits the size of a walnut very freely. These can be preserved in syrup. The plants are, however, expensive, but they are not difficult to keep with a winter minimum of 7–10°C (45–50°·F). A cool conservatory is ideal. They are not suitable for warm rooms with poor ventilation, and low humidity. Give good light and spray overhead in summer. Reacts well to foliar feeding with a vitamin product (see page

37). Prefers an acid compost. Do not be afraid to cut back if a plant becomes straggly. Keep only slightly moist in winter. Flowers, which are waxy white, are strongly scented. Fruit in various stages of ripening can be left on the plant the year round. 13–20 cm (5–8 in) pots depending on plant size.

Cliva miniata (kaffir lily)
Huge umbels of large showy orange/salmon trumpet flowers in spring. Large strap-shaped foliage. The plants have fleshy roots and need at least 25 cm (10 in) pots. They will survive little more than frost free conditions and are good for a porch or other cool place, but frost will blacken the foliage. A striking plant for a conservatory and extremely easy. Water well when growing, but keep almost dry over winter if the temperature is low.

Cyperus alternifolius (umbrella grass)
Foliage borne on long stems like the spines of an umbrella. It is semi-aquatic and is an easy plant for beginners since it is one of the few that will enjoy standing in water. Keep the compost quite moist at all times. Can be grown from seed. Minimum temperature about 10° C (50° F). Good light. At least 13 cm (5 in) pots.

Euonymus japonica
This is a garden shrub having very dwarf forms with attractive variegated foliage suitable for small pots. It is particularly useful for its hardy nature and the plant will tolerate even freezing and draughty places, such as an open porch. Buy 'Microphylla' forms from garden centres.

Euphorbia pulcherrima (poinsettia)
This is included because its popularity demands, rather than because its culture is easy. In most places with a cold climate its life is limited. The coloured bold bracts in pink, red, or white, make it a favourite Christmas plant, but after being bought it must be kept at a fairly constant 15.5–18.5° C (60–65° F) and in a bright position, if its condition is to be kept good for as long as possible. Plants produced for the florists are usually specially treated with dwarfing chemicals and daylight control. If you do save a plant it may not remain compact or produce its bracts at the same time the following year.

Fatshedera lizei
A hybrid between *Fatsia japonica* (below) and a *Hedera* (ivy) variety and

Sinningia speciosa is better known as Gloxinia and bears clusters of large flowers in striking colours.

having characters of both. At first growth is erect but later tends to sprawl unless supported. There is a cream variegated form. A good plant for shady cool conditions 13–18 cm (5–7 in) pots.

Fatsia japonica

This is sometimes wrongly called castor oil plant because the foliage resembles that of *Ricinus communis* in shape. When young, fatsia makes a tropical looking pot plant with its large shiny palmate foliage. It will eventually become too large and can be planted out since it is perfectly hardy. There is a variegated form with cream splashed and flecked leaves. It is a very useful plant for cold draughty places such as hallways and porches. 18–25 cm (7–10 in) pots according to plant size. Ricinus, the true castor oil, can be grown from seed and striking reddish leaved varieties can be obtained (see page 64).

Ferns

These are among the most beautiful and graceful of foliage plants, but unfortunately often deteriorate in the home. There are a vast number, but the most successful are those liking cool conditions. The delicately structured maidenhair ferns, Adiantum species, are probably best avoided, since they sometimes prove tricky. Fairly easy are *Pteris quadriaurita argyraea* which has a striking silvery variegated fronds, *Nephrolepsis exaltata* (ladder fern) which is impressive in a hanging basket but must not be allowed to dry out when it has lost its fronds in winter, *Athyrium filix-femina* (lady fern) and *Dryopteris filixmas* (male fern) – both quite hardy – *Polypedium vulgare* (adders fern, also hardy), and *Asplenium nidus* (bird's nest fern) with plain sword-shaped fronds. All these ferns like shade and a moist compost on the acid side.

Ficus (rubber plants)

Most popular *F. elastica* of which there are also cream and pale green variegated forms. Within reason these can be acclimatized to quite cool rooms, but a winter minimum of about 10° C (50° F) is advisable to prevent leaf deterioration and fall. *F. diversifolia* (mistletoe fig) which bears berry-like fruits, and *F. pumila* which can be grown as a trailer or a climber, both withstand far lower temperatures. If *F. elastica* becomes leggy by shedding lower leaves it can be rooted just below the healthy foliage by air layering (see page 82). Plenty of water when making active growth, only just moist at other times.

Fuchsia (ladies' ear-drops)

Although extremely popular fuchsias do not make good room plants and often shed flowers and foliage. They are ideal for conservatories, garden rooms, and porches, where conditions are cool, slightly shaded, and the air reasonably moist. Only frost-free conditions are needed in winter, but standard fuchsias need a minimum of about 10° C (50° F) to keep them just growing and to prevent die back of the head. Most plants can be trained by stopping the shoots. Plants should be well watered and fed when actively growing. Wide changes in conditions cause bud drop. For descriptions of the very many varieties and types a specialist catalogue should be consulted. 13 cm (5 in) pots, hanging containers, and pedestal pots.

Hedera (ivy)

There are a number of named varieties of *H. helix* which are practically hardy and also excellent where light is poor. The foliage may be attractively veined, frilled, or variegated with cream. *H. canariensis* has large leaves in a combination of green, pale green and cream, and can reach an impressive size if allowed. It is almost hardy, but should be gradually introduced to the cold. Pot size from 13–25 cm (5–10 in) for large *H canariensis* specimens. Some of the smaller ivies can be allowed to trail, but most need climbing support.

Helxine soleirolii (mind your own business)

A dainty carpeting plant with very invasive creeping tendency – hence common name. Likes plenty of water and considerable shade. Will often trail to completely cover a container, and can also be used to carpet compost surface in containers where other tall plants are growing. It is almost hardy but can be damaged by frost.

Hydrangea

This is often bought from a florist when in almost full bloom, and it should be given a cool shaded place to keep the flower heads in good condition for as long as possible. When the heads have faded, cut them cleanly from the plant together with any weak straggly growth. Stand outdoors in a shaded place with a pot preferably plunged to its rim in moist peat or sand. During summer cut away stems that have flowered to just above any fresh side shoots that form. These side shoots should produce flowers the following year. Keep the plants moist and give liquid feeds. In autumn, take the plant indoors and keep in a cool but frost-free place where there is plently of winter light but the temperature does not exceed about 10° C (50° F) If the temperature is higher, flowering may be inhibited. Repotting or potting-on can be done in late winter if required. Eventually plants may become too large to retain indoors and can then be planted out in the garden or in pots on a patio or balcony.

To get the best blue colour, special 'hydrangea colorant' preparations are sold. These should be dissolved in water or incorporated with the potting compost as directed on the label. An acid compost should always be used for potting, or chalk omitted from any compost you make yourself. Some varieties of hydrangea are naturally pink, red, or white. Do not attempt to turn these blue.

Maranta (prayer plant)
Several varieties of *M. leuconeura* are delightful foliage plants with oval leaves richly marked with chocolate spots or herringbone stripes. The leaves point upwards at night, hence the common name. However, they do not like cold and may become very tatty looking over the winter unless kept above about 10° C (50° F). Even so, plants that have suffered from cold usually grow away again with the return of warmer weather. Excellent for shaded places. Good humidity, 13 cm (5 in) pots.

Monstera (Swiss cheese plant)
M. deliciosa and *M. pertusa* are often sold as house plants with their names confused, but the latter has a more compact habit and rounded foliage. The foliage is large, shiny, sometimes variegated with cream, and holed or slitted. They are impressive where there is space such as in a hallway, but a winter minimum of about 10° C (50° F) is desirable. Large plants may need small tubs and strong cane supports. Plants form aerial roots and if these can be encouraged down to enter the pot, all the better. Give shade and moderate humidity. Water and feed when active growth is taking place in summer.

Nerium oleander
Shrubby plants with pointed glossy foliage and large clusters of single or double flowers in white or shades of red and pink. Almost hardy and will survive cold if kept on the dry side. Water very freely when growing in summer. Needs a 25 cm (10 in) pot and space to show its beauty. Excellent for a porch or conservatory. Flowers late spring to late summer very freely. Can be cut back to maintain size and shape. Good light or slight shade. Remove shoots that grow from base of flower trusses as soon as possible. The sap is poisonous.

Palms
Most of the tender florist's palms, such as the Howeias (Kentia) palms,

sometimes deteriorate in rooms. The hardy types grow too large. One you can raise yourself from seed sown in summer on a warm window sill is *Pheonix canariensis*, but this too is sold by houseplants shops and nurseries. It has a typical graceful palm shape and can be kept in pots for several years. It too will eventually become enormous and may have to be scrapped – hence the usefulness of being able to grow this species from seed easily. It is hardy in very mild parts of the south and west of the UK and reaches a great height. It is a good plant for a cool hallway or porch.

Peperomia

Peperomia species show a wide diversity of foliage shape and habit. With the exception of *P. sandersii* (which can be difficult) most make easy house plants. *P. glabella* and *P. scandens* are trailers. *P. caperata* is a small compact plant with crinkled foliage and erect creamy-white catkin-like flowers. *P. magnoliaefolia* has large oval green and cream variegated foliage. Be careful not to overwater or there may be basal rotting. Minimum temperature about 10° C (50° F). Slight shade.

Philodendron scandens

One of the easiest of the philodendrons, suitable for warm or cool rooms and of trailing habit. It can be trained upright if preferred, and can be given either a bright position or shade. The spade-shaped foliage is glossy with a bronze tint when young. About 13 cm (5 in) pots. Minimum temperature about 7° C (45° F).

Pilea cadierei (aluminium plant)

Charming house plant with dainty leaves beautifully marked silver. Sprinkle Epsom salts on the compost from time to time to prevent magnesium deficiency to which plants are prone, causing poor leaf colour and distortion. Water cautiously in winter, shade in summer. Minimum temperature about 10° C (50° F).

Plumbago capensis

This is really a wall shrub, but is often sold as a house plant trained up canes or around a wire hoop. The common form is blue, but there is a white. The flowers are phlox-like and freely borne spring to autumn. Excellent for a frost-free porch or conservatory or garden room, but best given space and a 25 cm (10 in) pot. Plants can be kept smaller by cutting back after flowering by two-thirds. It's easy from seed.

Rhoeo discolor vittatum

An attractive plant with strap-shaped foliage rosette fashion. The leaves are striped green and cream above and flushed deep rose underneath. Flowers form in cup-shape structures at the stem base but are curious rather than showy. Water cautiously in winter and give minimum of about 10° C (50° F). A vigorous plant produces offshoots that can be separated for propagation. Slight shade. 13 cm (5 in) pot.

Sansevieria trifasciata laurentii (snake plant)

Fairly well-known foliage plant with tall erect variegated sword-shaped leaves. It has a reputation of being difficult, but failure is nearly always due to overwatering. It can be left for long periods without water and in winter hardly any should be given. It can be propagated in summer from leaf cuttings (see page 79) but is unlikely to give plants with the same variegation. Good light. Winter minimum about 10–13° C (50–55° F).

Schizanthus 'Hit Parade' is a neat and easy quick flowering plant to grow from seed.

Saxifraga sarmentosa (mother of thousands)

A popular house plant for hanging containers or pedestals. The foliage has cream veins giving a marbled effect above, and a purplish flush below. Long runners with plantlets at the ends are freely produced – hence common name. Almost hardy and good for cool shady places.

Setcreasea purpurea

This plant is rather like aspidistra for resistance to neglect. Plants have been found in empty houses and revived after being forgotten for many months. It is a trailing plan with elongated slightly woolly foliage or glorious purple colour. If the stems are stopped it can be encouraged to grow more bushy and upright which reduces the tendency to straggle. It will tolerate shade but develops a richer colour in good light. Small magenta-coloured flowers are produced but these are not showy.

Stephanotis floribunda

One of the more expensive and exotic house plants usually bought trained around a wire hoop. It has dark green shiny foliage and clusters of tubular waxy white highly fragrant flowers from summer to early autumn. With care it can be acclimatized to relatively cool conditions, but deterioration occurs if winter minimum falls below about 10° C (50° F). In winter keep just moist and in summer water and feed freely, giving overhead spraying with water from time to time to keep up humidity. Can be trained up canes. At lease 13 cm (5 in) pot depending on plant size.

Tradescantia (wandering Jew)

Several forms of this well-known house plant exist, but they are often not seen at their best due to being given dark position. In good light the fine tints and colours are developed. Taking care not to overwater also helps. A fine species is *T. blossfeldiana* which has rose pink flowers from early spring to late summer. It is best in a hanging basket, but likes slight shade and good humidity. Winter minimum about 10° C (50° F).

Zebrina pendula

Often called a 'tradescantia' this species is of similar habit. The most common variety is 'Quadricolor' with foliage striped with silvery white and shades of green and pink above, purple below. This also needs good light to develop full colours. However, other varieties may prefer shade and with this plant it is wise to experiment with positions to find the best for leaf colour. Again colour is also affected by overwatering which tends to cause fading.

Chapter 7

Simple Propagation

Propagation from seed has been described in Chapter 5, but several other types of simple propagation can be done on a window sill. You can propagate to obtain fresh young stock if a plant is becoming too large or 'leggy' with age, or if a plant is accidentally damaged, or just because you want more plants for yourself or for friends. However, never use plants for propagation if they appear sickly from some unidentified cause. Particularly avoid plants showing mottling, distortion, stunting, or striping and disfigurement of flowers. These symptoms could mean virus disease for which there is no cure. Propagation can pass the trouble on, and insects can also pass the disease from one plant to another. Even handling affected plants can spread infection, so they are best destroyed.

If a plant has been damaged and perhaps had its appearance spoiled by pest attack and the pest has been satisfactorily controlled, there is no objection to propagation.

STEM CUTTINGS

Shoots of most plants will root if cut off, properly prepared, and inserted in a rooting compost. It is done as follows. Select a healthy shoot carrying several leaves, and cut it cleanly from the plant. The shoot need be only several inches long and will depend on the plant size and type. Large cuttings are unnecessary and are more difficult to root. Remove the leaves from the lower part of the stem and cut off the remains of the lower stem from immediately under where the leaves were attached – this point is called a 'node'. Use a sharp knife or razor blade to make the cut below the node, so as not to bruise the tissue. It is from this point that roots will subsequently form (Fig. 34).

The next stage is to insert the cutting in a rooting compost (Fig. 35). A simple one is a mixture of equal parts of moss peat and washed grit, but you can use any of the proprietary seed and cutting composts now sold in shops. The rooting mixture can be put in a pot or in a seed tray if a lot of cuttings are taken. If a pot is used the cuttings usually root more easily if they are inserted around the edge. Insert the cuttings

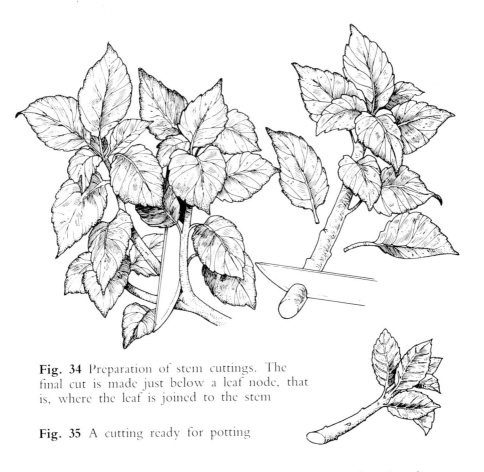

Fig. 34 Preparation of stem cuttings. The final cut is made just below a leaf node, that is, where the leaf is joined to the stem

Fig. 35 A cutting ready for potting

firmly making sure the mixture is nicely moist, but keeping the upper foliage away from the compost surface. It is now necessary to keep in moisture and prevent the leaves of the cuttings losing moisture and wilting. If this happens the cuttings may die before they get a chance to form roots to take in moisture from the compost.

A transparent polythene bag makes an excellent cover for a pot, or a seed tray of cuttings can be slipped inside one, the polythene being kept clear of the foliage by a home-made wire support. Special flowerpots with transparent dome can be bought for window sill propagation, also trays with covers. Another simple way of rooting is to put the cutting in a plastic bag at the bottom of which is placed the rooting compost. The bag can then be pegged to a line strung across a window or supported similarly. The roots when formed can be seen through the polythene.

Rooting takes place more rapidly in a warm position, but the hardier the plant the less warmth necessary. The cuttings should have plenty of diffused light – but they must be put out of direct sunshine. Warmth does not mean excessive heat, such as over a radiator. Most plants in this book will give cuttings rooting well at from 16–21° C (60–70° F).

A good time to take cuttings is in spring when the plants are usually about to make vigorous growth. Autumn may also be suitable.

Make sure you keep the rooting compost moist, but as soon as roots have formed transfer the cutting to a potting compost containing the nutrients necessary for proper growth. Use only a small pot large enough to take the cutting comfortably in the early stage, and pot-on to larger pots as growth proceeds (see page 28).

LEAF CUTTINGS

Leaves can often be made to sprout roots if they are suitably prepared (Fig. 36). This technique is particularly used for plants of the begonia and gesneria families and has been mentioned in the plant descriptions in Chapter 6.

Small leaves like, for example, those of saintpaulias and peperomias, can often be detached whole and inserted at the stalk end in a cutting compost as described for stem cuttings. Roots will grow from the stalk and a new plant arise. The original parent leaf usually withers eventually when the new plant is established. Large leaves can be cut in small pieces. Elongated leaves like those of streptocarpus or sansevieria, can be cut into several sections of about 5 cm (2 in) in length. Roundish leaves, or large spade-shaped ones like *Begonia rex*, can be cut up into several triangular sections. In this case cut out triangles from around the edge so that a leaf vein comes at the apex of each triangle. When the triangles are inserted in the cutting compost see that the leaf vein angle is immersed.

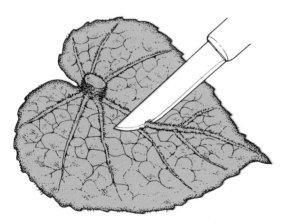

Fig. 36 Preparing a leaf cutting by slitting veins

Some leaves will root if they are detached, the leaf being cut at intervals on the underside, and just rested on the surface of the cutting compost or gently weighted down with pieces of clean broken clay pot. A single leaf so treated may give several plants—one at each point where the leaf vein is cut (Fig. 37).

Leaf cuttings, like stem cuttings, must be covered with a transparent enclosure to keep in moisture, and they too will root faster if a slightly warm place is found for them.

Fig. 37 A rooted leaf cutting

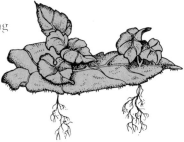

DIVISION

Pot plants that grow as a clump, rather than as a single stem can be propagated simply by dividing the roots when potting-on or repotting. The best time to do this is when the plants are about to make new growth, usually early spring. If the roots are very tangled and matted, or if they are tuberous, less damage will be done if they are divided with a very sharp knife (Fig. 38). Pulling apart may crush tissues which may later rot. After dividing a plant water sparingly at first, until it is seen that the plant is making new roots. This will be apparent by strong healthy top growth forming.

Fig. 38 Increasing a plant by division

Plants with well-defined tubers, corms, or similar storage organs, can usually be propagated by cutting up so that each piece has an 'eye' or growing shoot. The best way to do this is to immerse the storage organs in moist peat in a warm place when it is time to start them into growth – again usually early spring. Shoots will soon appear and they can then be cut up easily. To avoid tissue damage use a very sharp blade, such as a razor, and dust the cut surface with powdered charcoal before potting. Again water sparingly at first and until vigorous growth begins.

OFFSETS

This is the name given to the tiny bulblets that sometimes form around the large mother bulb during growth. The offsets can be separated at repotting time and potted in small pots individually. These little bulbs may take several years to become large enough to produce flowers, but the method of propagation is far quicker than from seed (Fig. 39). Other storage organs such as tubers and rhizomes may multiply during a growing season and can be separated when it is time to restart them into growth.

Fig. 39 Bulbs can be increased from offsets, though these will not flower for a few years

LAYERING

This method is used for climbing and trailing plants, such as ivies, some of which readily form roots on the stems even in the air. Choose a suitably long stem and pull it down so that part of it can be pegged to the surface of a cutting compost contained in a separate small pot. Where the stem contacts the compost it may assist rapid rooting if a leaf is removed or the stem is slit and the compost is just allowed to cover this point. A piece of wire bent to form a U shape can be used as a staple to keep the stem in place (Fig. 40). When rooting has occurred the stem can be severed from the parent plant.

Fig. 40 Layering a trailing plant – slitting the stem where it touches the compost will speed rooting

AIR LAYERING

This is a useful technique for plants that become leggy and plants that through some misfortune lose their lower foliage, such as the rubber plant, *Ficus elastica*. The operation is best done during summer when there is plenty of natural warmth.

At the point of the stem where you want new roots to form, just under the existing foliage, make an upward slit in the stem. In this wedge slip a small piece of fibrous peat dusted with hormone rooting powder, see below, and wrap around this some moist sphagnum moss mixed with peat and a little grit. Cover the whole with a band of

Fig. 41 Air layering is a simple method of propagation

transparent polythene securing at the top and bottom with tape, or florists' wire if care is taken not to cut into the stem (Fig. 41). All you have to do then is to wait until roots can be seen through the polythene, remove the wrapping of polythene and pot the rooted top of the plant after severing just below where the new roots have formed. Do not remove the moss/peat mixture from around the roots before potting. The roots will soon grow out into the potting compost.

ROOTING HORMONES

Several preparations are sold to stimulate rooting. These may aid the rooting of plants that are likely to form roots from cuttings, but have little effect on obstinate cases. The hormones are certainly worth trying and can be obtained in the powder and liquid form and recently, as a gel or jelly. Dip the end of the cutting in the preparation before insertion into the rooting powder (Fig. 42). Some preparations have a fungicide added to reduce risk of the cutting rotting. Full instructions for use are always given on the label.

Fig. 42 Using a rooting hormone

CHAPTER 8

SPECIAL TECHNIQUES AND AIDS

AUTOMATIC WATERING, HUMIDITY, AND TEMPERATURE

Apart from the automatic watering pots described on page 20, some more elaborate aids to cope with a group of plants can be obtained. These can be used when you want to leave plants for some time. Simple and convenient is the capillary sand bench, the modern forms of which use a lightweight porous plastic matting in place of messy sand. This capillary matting can also be used to stand plants on, and to maintain humidity, in plant windows or in trays on an ordinary window sill. So that the plants can take up moisture from the sand or matting, they must be given uncrocked (see page 32) pots, but a tuft of peat, or glass wool as used for heat insulation, can be used instead to keep the compost in the pot (Fig. 43). The pots must be firmly pressed onto the capillary surface so that moisture can flow upwards through the drainage hole and into the compost. Provided the capillary material is kept moist this flow will be automatic and will increase as the plant uses up the compost moisture.

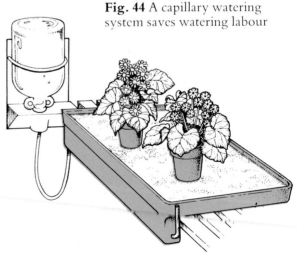

Fig. 44 A capillary watering system saves watering labour

Fig. 43 Pots to stand on capillary matting should have wide drainage holes, and should not be crocked

To keep the capillary material supplied with water the simplest arrangement is an inverted reservoir bottle (Fig. 44), but some benches can be connected to a mains water supply and have a constant level float valve. The piping for connection is one eighth inch bore and little thicker than an electric cable. The benches are usually plastic and in the form of trays which can be connected together to increase the area of the system at any time if desired. A snag with this arrangement is that it is more difficult to disguise flowerpots, and it is not always easy to find ornamental containers with suitable drainage holes. Plastic or unglazed drained containers are suitable, clay pots are not. Of course capillary trays and benches will maintain humidity automatically even if plants are stood on them without the added benefit of taking up root moisture.

A little extra artificial warmth – even enough to keep the temperature from falling below freezing – may be a great advantage, for example in a plant window or a bay-type window where there's lots of glass. For this purpose electric heating tubes or even a small fan heater as used for greenhouses could be employed (Fig. 45). Thermostatic control with a separate thermostat will ensure economical use of electricity. If a fan heater is used it must not be one of the continuous blowing type. The fan should operate only when the heat is switched on by the thermostat. A rod type thermostat is the most accurate and in the long run saves its extra cost by reducing the electricity bill.

Fig. 45 A small thermostatically controlled fan heater can protect your plants in cold weather.

THERMOMETERS AND HYGROMETERS

A maximum and minimum thermometer put among your plants is a great help in arranging temperature conditions to suit them. This type of thermometer has two scales, each having a movable indicator resting on top of the mercury column (Fig. 46a). The indicators can be set with a magnet or on some thermometer designs by pressing a button or

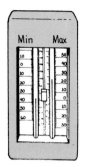

Fig. 46 A maximum/ minimum thermometer is very useful. *Right:* A hygrometer

swivelling. The indicators show the lowest temperature that has been attained on one scale and the maximum on the other. Thus during an absence you can see on return how the temperature has varied.

Also useful is a direct reading hygrometer which shows the degree of humidity in the air. Most are calibrated in percent relative humidity, but the simplest types also have the conditions 'dry', 'moist', and 'wet' indicated (Fig. 46b).

DWARFING PLANTS

Many plants can be kept compact or dwarfed by training. The growing of Bonsai (miniature Japanese trees), which are not good permanent house plants, is covered by many specialist books which should be consulted for information.

A special dwarfing technique is treatment with certain chemicals. The one most used is Cycocel. A solution of this, made according to the supplier's directions (see Appendix), is either watered into the plant or poured over as a drench. This chemical is safe to use if reasonable precautions are taken, but has not yet been cleared for edible crops, although it has been experimentally used on them. It usually reduces the stem parts of plants having little effect on flower or leaf size, but not all plants respond to treatment.

GROWING PLANTS IN CASES AND BOTTLES

Where homes are centrally heated and the air dry, or when plants have to be left for long periods without attention, closed cases or large bottles make an excellent environment (Fig. 47). The practice of growing in glass cases was introduced as long ago as the early nineteenth century by Nathaniel Bagshaw Ward. Cases of glass or plastic on legs, or large glass bottles like carboys or demijohns, are

Cordyline, Saintpaulia, begonia, and pteris ferns give a pleasing combination of foliage with flowers.

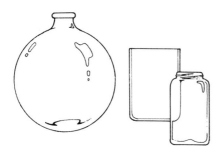

Fig. 47 Many plants will grow well in bottles or jars

usually used today. Covered fish tanks, battery jars, and large sweet jars, also make good and attractive homes for suitable plants. Such containers can be practically sealed and hardly any moisture is lost from the compost or by transpiration from the plant foliage. This means they keep fresh for long periods and little watering attention is needed.

Most plants can be kept in these enclosures provided those chosen all, more or less, like the same conditions of temperature and light, and remain suitably low-growing or small and compact. Rampant fast growers are utterly unsuitable and will soon swamp all other plants in the container.

Some plant suggestions are as follows: *Aregelia carolinae*, *Cryptanthus aculis rubra*, *C. bivittatus*, *Vriesia splendens major* (all bromeliads, see page 67), *Calathea lubbersiana*, *Davallia mariessii* (dainty small fern, but not evergreen), *Fittonia argyroneura* (beautiful lace-like leaf veining, difficult outside cases and bottles), marantas (see page 73), many peperomia species (see page 74), *Pilea cadierei* for larger cases (see page 74), *Tetranema mexicanum* (Mexican foxglove, grow from seed), small orchids of the 'slipper' type (paphiopedilums).

The compost put in the containers should not be too rich. John Innes No. 1 mixed with some extra grit and some crushed charcoal added are suitable, or any other proprietary brand similarly diluted. This is to keep growth as slow as possible. The containers should be planted with artistic effect and small pieces of natural stone can be incorporated if desired. Bank the compost so that it slopes up to the rear of the container.

With narrow-necked bottles use a paper funnel to introduce compost so as to avoid soiling the sides. Use a pair of flattish sticks to lower plants into place and a cotton reel on a stick to firm them in position. For cutting off surplus growth and removing faded leaves a razor blade on a stick and a piece of sharp steel knitting needle are useful (Fig.48).

Bottle and case gardens are best where the temperature is moderate

Fig. 48 Tools for planting a bottle

and with a winter minimum of about 10° C (50° F) also where it is slightly shaded. Conditions which are too cold will encourage excessive condensation which will obscure the plants from view. For bottles a tuft of cotton wool makes a convenient closure allowing some air change but keeping out pests and diseases. Bottle gardens can sometimes be fitted with gallery, lamp, and shade, to make an attractive table lamp. The extra artificial light in the evenings will be beneficial to the plants.

ARTIFICIAL LIGHT

This can be a great aid to house plant health, and it can also make possible the growing of plants in otherwise impossible gloomy places. The best general type of illumination is the fluorescent tube where house plants are concerned. Special plant troughs on legs with shaded tubes fitted can be purchased for growing African violets. Some people may be able to make up their own illumination systems, but in all cases care is needed to comply with full electrical safety regulations.

Fluorescent tubes usually need to be set between 45–60 cm (18–24 in) above the tops of plants for adequate illumination. It is possible to obtain special tubes for plant irradiation and tubes that are designed to show colours truly without abnormal distortions (full spectrum True-lite tubes). Under the light from some tubes blue and red colours can look remarkably drab. Most fluorescent tubes give out a gentle warmth that plants will enjoy. Ordinary filament lamps are rarely suitable. They produce too much heat and need to be put too close to give adequate illumination.

Unless the position is exceptionally dark, lighting need be switched on only for a few hours each day to give extra light that will benefit the plants. If preferred a time switch can be fitted. Plants may not react well to continuous light and this may upset the flowering, or even inhibit it, in plants grown for their blooms. However, most low-growing plants will enjoy artificial light, those belonging to the African violet family (the gesneriads) doing especially well. These include gloxinias, streptocarpus (of which the John Innes hybrids are especially recommended), Smithiantha hybrids, gesneria or rechsteineria, achimenes, and aeschynanthus. Peperomias and marantas also grow exceptionally well. Tall plants are unlikely to benefit much. Light falls off in intensity quite dramatically as the distance from the source of illumination is increased. Although the growing tips of tall plants may be getting enough of the artificial light the greater part of the rest may receive a worthless amount. It is not easy to reach the intensity of daylight artificially without appreciable cost. For suppliers of special lighting equipment see Appendix.

APPENDIX

TO MAKE A LARGE BUCKETFUL OF JOHN INNES COMPOST

First find an empty household plastic bottle and pour in 760 cm³ (26¾ fl oz) of water. Mark off the level and cut off the bottle above that point leaving a measure holding the specified volume. Use this, filled level with the top, to measure out volumes of peat, loam and grit, as follows:

N.B. The weighing of small quantities of fertilizers can be conveniently done with a small diabetic balance available from most large pharmacists.

SEED COMPOST (about one-third bucketful)

Two measures of sterilized loam, one measure of best quality moss peat, and one measure of clean washed sand. To this add 9.5 g (1/3 oz) calcium superphosphate and 5.5 g (1/5 oz) chalk. Mix together thoroughly.

POTTING COMPOST NO. 1 (large bucketful)

Seven measures sterilized loam, three measures of medium moss peat, two measures washed grit. To this add 28 g (1 oz) John Innes Base Fertilizer and 5.5 g (1/5 oz) chalk. If No. 2 potting compost is required double the amount of fertilizer and chalk, treble for No. 3 and so on. Higher than No. 2 is rarely needed. Remember to omit chalk for lime-hating plants.

TO STERILIZE LOAM

Boil 1 cm (½ in) of water in a domestic saucepan and add dry sifted good garden soil (if proper loam is unavailable) nearly to the brim. Simmer this mixture for 15 minutes and then turn out on a clean surface to cool.

(Note: soil or loam is sometimes sold already sterilized by some nurseries, so ask around.)

Narcissus 'Golden Harvest'. Inexpensive bulbs to give a wealth of brilliant colour.

UNIVERSITY OF CALIFORNIA COMPOSTS

First mix equal volumes of best quality peat and washed sand or grit.

U.C. seed compost   To each large bucketful of the above mixture add: 3.5 g (1/8 oz) ammonium sulphate, 7 g (¼ oz) calcium superphosphate, just under 7 g (¼ oz) potassium sulphate, and 28 g (1 oz) chalk.

U.C. potting compost   To each large bucketful of peat/grit mix add: 21 g (¾ oz) ammonium nitrate, 7 g (¼ oz) potassium sulphate, 21 g (¾ oz) hoof and horn, 14 g (½ oz) magnesium limestone, 28 g (1 oz) chalk, and 14 g (½ oz) calcium superphosphate.

SUPPLIERS OF CHEMICALS, FERTILIZERS, AND PACKS OF FERTILIZERS FOR COMPOST MIXES

Chempak Products, Geddings Road, Hoddesdon, Herts, EN11 0LR; (also supply Cycocel for dwarfing and other chemicals). Phostrogen: products available from most garden shops and centres.

PLANTSMEN

A very wide range of house plants is now sold by high-class florists, supermarkets, and stores like Marks & Spencer, and garden centres. B. Wall, 4 Selbourne Close, New Haw, Weybridge, Surrey (foliage begonia and bromeliad specialist, also other popular house plants). Long Man Gardens, Lewes Road, Wilmington, Polegate, East Sussex, BN26 5RS, (wide range of indoor and conservatory plants). Holly Gate Nurseries Ltd, Billingshurst Lane, Ashington, Sussex, (cacti and other succulents) Efenechtyd Nurseries, Efenechtyd, Ruthin, Clwyd, (streptocarpus specialist).

BULBS AND OTHER STORAGE ORGANS

P. de Jager and Sons Ltd, Marden, Kent. Walter Blom & Son Ltd, Leavesden, Watford, Hertfordshire. Blackmore & Langden Ltd, Bath, Somerset, (begonias, gloxinias, etc.). Nerine Nurseries, Welland, Worcestershire, (nerine specialists). K. J. Townsend, 17 Valerie Close, St Albans, Hertfordshire, AL1 5JD, (achimenes specialist).

AUTOMATIC AIDS AND GADGETS

Thermoforce Ltd, Camplex Plant Care Division, Heybridge Works, Maldon, Essex, CM9 5NW. Humex, Gore Road Industrial Estate, New Milton, Hampshire, BH25 6SF.

PEAT AND POTTING COMPOSTS

A very wide selection of ready-made composts with brand names is now available from garden centres and shops.

ARTIFICIAL LIGHTING EQUIPMENT

Sunlight Systems, Unit 154, Stratford Workshops, Burford Road, London, E15 2SP. Sungro-Lite Ltd, 118 Chatsworth Road, Willesden Green, London, NW2 5QU. Thermoforce Ltd, Camplex Plant Care Division, Heybridge Works, Maldon, Essex, CM9 5NW. Wotan Lamps Ltd, Wotan House, 1 Gresham Way, Durnsford Road, London, SW19 8HU. Full Spectrum True-Lite, S.M.L. Unit 4, Wye Estate, London Road, High Wycombe, Bucks, (suppliers of full spectrum True-Lite fluorescent tubes). Humex, Gore Road Industrial Estate, New Milton, Hampshire, BH25 6SF.

UNITED STATES SUPPLIERS

CHEMICALS, FERTILIZERS, PESITICIDES
Science Products Company, Inc, 2640 N. Greenview Avenue, Chicago, Illinois 60614

SEEDSMEN (also general nurserymen and suppliers of sundries and house plants)
W. Atlee Burpee Co, Warminster, Pa, 18974.

PLANTSMEN AND HOUSE PLANT SUPPLIERS
House Plant Corner, Box 155-H, Oxford, Maryland 21654. Guaranteed Plant Club, Box 66GF, Robbinsville, N.J. 08691. Wyrtzen Exotic Plants, 165 Bryant Avenue, Floral Park, N.Y. Roehrs Co, Box 125, E. Rutherford, N.J.L. Easterbrook, 10 Craig Street, Butler, Ohio. Merry Gardens, Camden, Main.

BULBS, ETC.

Rockwood Gardens, 134 Weston S.W., Grand Rapids, Michigan 49502. P. de Jager & Sons Inc, SO. Hamilton, Ma. 01982. International Growers Exchange, Box 397-C, Farmington, Michigan 48024.

GROWING AIDS, ARTIFICIAL LIGHTING, ETC.

General Electric, Nela Park, Cleveland, Ohio. Sylvania, 100 Endicott Street, Danvers, Mass.

INDEX